knit along with

DEBBIE MACOMBER
A Charity Guide for Knitters

LEISURE ARTS, INC.
Little Rock, Arkansas

EDITORIAL STAFF

Editor-in-Chief: Susan White Sullivan
Knit and Crochet Publications Director: Debra Nettles
Special Projects Director: Susan Frantz Wiles
Senior Prepress Director: Mark Hawkins
Art Publications Director: Rhonda Shelby
Technical Editor: Cathy Hardy
Contributing Editors: Sarah J. Green and Lois J. Long
Editorial Writer: Susan McManus Johnson
Art Category Manager: Lora Puls
Graphic Artist: Amy Temple
Production Artist: Janie Wright
Imaging Technicians: Brian Hall, Stephanie Johnson,
     and Mark R. Potter
Photography Manager: Katherine Atchison
Contributing Photographers: Jason Masters
     and Mark Mathews
Contributing Photo Stylists: Angela Alexander
     and Christy Myers
Publishing Systems Administrator: Becky Riddle
Publishing Systems Assistants: Clint Hanson
     and John Rose

BUSINESS STAFF

Vice President and Chief Operations Officer:
     Tom Siebenmorgen
Director of Finance and Administration:
     Laticia Mull Dittrich
Vice President, Sales and Marketing:
     Pam Stebbins
National Accounts Director: Martha Adams
Sales and Services Director: Margaret Reinold
Information Technology Director: Hermine Linz
Controller: Francis Caple
Vice President, Operations: Jim Dittrich
Comptroller, Operations: Rob Thieme
Retail Customer Service Manager: Stan Raynor
Print Production Manager: Fred F. Pruss

Instructions tested and photo models made by JoAnn
Bowling, Susan Carter, Sue Galucki, Raymelle Greening,
Dale Potter, Margaret Taverner, and Ted Tomany.

Library of Congress Control Number: 2009929768
ISBN-13: 978-1-60140-232-5
ISBN-10: 1-60140-232-5

10 9 8 7 6 5 4 3 2

contents

debbie macomber

photo by Nina Subin

Dear Friends,

Of all the *Knit Along with Debbie Macomber* books, I think this one is my favorite. I probably say that about every book, but there is something truly special about *A Charity Guide for Knitters*.

I've been a big fan of knitting charities for a long time now, and I've seen the wonderful things that knitters accomplish because of their generous hearts.

How about you—does the idea of making a baby blanket for a child who is ill make you want to grab your knitting needles and get busy? Do you run a mental inventory of your yarn stash when you hear that a homeless man needs a blanket or a woman undergoing chemotherapy needs a hat? I bet you do, because hearing about people in need makes me want to get busy, too. We knitters know we can make a difference, and that's why I'm so excited about this book.

In fact, by purchasing any *Knit Along with Debbie Macomber* book or any product from the Knit Along with Debbie Macomber Collection, you are already helping others. That's because I donate my proceeds from sales of these items to my favorite charities, including Warm Up America! and World Vision. Visit TheLeisureBoutique.com to see all these fun pattern books and helpful products.

Drop by DebbieMacomber.com the next time you're online, and let me know what you knit for charity. I look forward to hearing from you!

Debbie

If there isn't a Binky Patrol chapter near you, you can send finished blankets to:

Binky Patrol, Inc.
c/o Carolyn Berndt
19065 Ridgeview Rd.
Villa Park, CA 92861

www.binkypatrol.org

Pattern Suggestions:

Baby Blanket
(page 58)

Afghan
(page 60)

Binky Patrol, Inc.

Security Blankets for Children in Distress

Children shouldn't know what it's like to be sick or afraid. Yet all too often, babies and youngsters do experience serious illness, abuse, abandonment, or homelessness. However, there are organizations like Binky Patrol that make it their mission to help provide comfort and warmth to children experiencing trauma of any kind.

Since its inception in 1996, Binky Patrol's goal of helping children in need has won the hearts of an estimated 20,000 volunteers who knit, crochet, quilt, and sew. Together, these groups of selfless individuals have created many thousands of blankets called "binkies" for children from ages newborn to eighteen years. The organization has more than 160 chapters of blanket-makers nationwide, which are easy to locate on the Binky Patrol Web site, **www.binkypatrol.org**.

The Web site also has helpful ideas for getting your church, school, or other group involved in making binkies, including a no-sew fleece blanket. There are lists of upcoming Binky Patrol events, such as the annual Bink-A-Thon involving volunteers from several states who gather to make as many blankets as they can in a single day.

While you visit the Web site, be sure to read the heartwarming stories shared by volunteers and the parents of binky recipients. You will see how the gift of one warm blanket for a child can also lend reassurance to a worried parent.

Binky Patrol, Inc. is a 501(c)(3) not-for-profit organization meeting the standards of the National Charities Information Bureau. As founder Susan Finch says, "We make blankets and give them away to children in need of comfort. It's as simple as that."

Children in Common

Taking Handmade Comforts to Russia's Orphans

Children in Common
A Humanitarian Program of Adoptions Together

For the estimated 750,000 children living in Russia's orphanages, clothing and medicine are often in short supply. Many of the buildings are old and lack adequate heat. The government supplies a minimum of clothing. For some, the food is poor in nutrition. Even baths are infrequent, as many orphanages do not have hot water. The administrators of these facilities do all that they can for the children, but there is little help available to alleviate the bleakness of the orphans' lives.

American Karen Porter saw these dismal conditions firsthand while in Russia to adopt a child. As a result, she and Janice Pearse, another adoptive mom, founded Children in Common in 1992 (CIC is now administered as a charitable program of Adoptions Together). In 1998, Karen responded wholeheartedly to a mission trip, knitting 144 wool hats for the children to add to the clothing, medical supplies, toys and educational materials the group delivered. When this incredible number wasn't nearly enough, she began recruiting other knitters to create warm articles of clothing for children ages newborn to sixteen years. Since then, parents traveling to Russia to adopt have included hand knit wool items in their suitcases for the orphans. These days, smaller items are preferred because of baggage restrictions.

The organization also alerts volunteers and donors to the resources needed to improve the health, living conditions, and vocational training of orphans in Russia and Lithuania. CIC funds programs that teach the older children to sew and knit for themselves—skills that can help support them when they leave orphanage care. Vist the "Current Projects" and "How You Can Help" pages of **www.adoptionstogether.org/common** or **www.childrenincommon.org** to learn more.

If you can knit wool socks, gloves, or other small garments or accessories for the orphans, please send them to:

Children In Common
Adoptions Together, Inc.
5750 Executive Dr.,
Suite 107
Baltimore, MD 21228

www.childrenincommon.org

Pattern Suggestions:

Cuffed Hat
(page 17)

Hooded Scarf
(page 24)

Mittens
(page 27)

Thick Socks
(page 32)

Infant's Pullover
(page 42)

Finished garments should be sent to:

Christmas at Sea
The Seamen's
Church Institute
241 Water Street
New York, NY 10038

www.seamenschurch.org

Pattern Suggestions:

Cuffed Hat
(page 17)

Helmet Liner
(page 20)

Scarf
(page 26)

Socks
(page 34)

Mariner's Vest
(page 54)

Bulky Sweater
(page 64)

Christmas at Sea
Warming Mariners' Hearts with Handmade Gifts

For more than 100 years, the Seaman's Church Institute (SCI) has delivered gifts to the world's mariners through its *Christmas at Sea* and *Christmas on the River* programs. Due to the generosity and creative efforts of volunteers who live in every state of the nation, SCI typically distributes 17,000 hand-knitted and crocheted garments. These gifts bring holiday cheer and comfort to the personnel of international cargo ships and towboats on America's inland waterways.

The handmade scarves, caps, sweaters, vests, socks, and helmets arrive at SCI Headquarters in New York City throughout the year, where *Christmas at Sea* Program Director Jeanette DeVita oversees the sorting of these very special gifts.

Participants in the program are asked to use yarn that can be laundered by machine. Worsted or medium weight yarn is used for all garments except socks, which should be knitted with sport weight yarn. Since most mariners are men, the use of pastel colors is discouraged. For variety, variegated, ombré, tweed, or flecked yarns are acceptable.

Individuals who are prevented from participating because they live on a fixed income may call the Seamen's Church Institute at 212-349-9090 to receive yarn at no cost. SCI also has yarn available for purchase, and currently suggests a donation of $2.50 per skein.

SCI is happy to receive the knitted garments for its *Christmas at Sea* and *Christmas on the River* programs January through December, yet finds it most helpful to receive donations in the fall when gift packing begins.

Please visit **www.seamenschurch.org** and click on "How You Can Help" for more information about SCI, the latest on *Christmas at Sea* goals, and updates to knitting guidelines. While there, read the *Christmas at Sea* blog to learn how your knitted gifts can brighten the holiday for mariners.

Newborns in Need, Inc.

Welcoming Babies with Warmth and Love

Serving All God's Children

Started in Houston, Missouri in 1992 and now headquartered in Pfafftown, North Carolina, Newborns in Need provides basic essentials to hospitals and social service agencies that provide assistance to premature, ill, or impoverished newborns. By dedicating their time, talents and love, NIN volunteers are able to give a warm welcome to at-risk newborns in their own local communities. Utilizing their sewing, crocheting, or knitting skills to create much-needed items, volunteers participate in The Largest Baby Shower on the Planet during the month of May. They invite beginners to join in, and enlist their help year-round in collecting donations and supplies to support their local chapter. Clothing, diapers, blankets, hats, and many other basic items are donated to these little ones.

Sadly, some babies lose their fight for life. Hospitals find that the grieving family appreciates the ability to hold their baby son or daughter, dressed in specially crafted gowns and wrapped in a beautiful blanket, as they struggle to say their final good-byes.

"I can't imagine a more tragic event in anyone's life than to lose a child," says Connie Edwards, National President of Newborns in Need. "I consider it an honor that our organization provides an outfit and blanket acknowledging the baby's life, no matter what the gestational age."

As of early 2009, the organization supports 52 volunteer chapters and is opening new chapters when leaders come forward. If you knit, sew, crochet, or quilt, or if you can lead a group who will support babies in your area, visit **www.newbornsinneed.org** or contact **nationaloffice@newbornsinneed.org** to locate a volunteer chapter near you. The organization is a 501(c)(3) charity, providing tax deductible receipts when requested. Call 1-877-231-5097 to learn how you can become a Newborns in Need volunteer.

To locate a volunteer chapter of Newborns in Need in your area, visit

www.newbornsinneed.org

or call
1-877-231-5097

Pattern Suggestion:

Baby Blanket
(page 58)

Operation Helmetliner

Helping America's Servicemen Defeat the Cold

In December of 2004, Bob and Linda Swinford of Illinois learned of the sub-zero temperatures sometimes endured by American military personnel. Linda immediately knitted a wool helmet liner for a family friend stationed in Iraq, who said, "It has certainly been a help, or should I say 'a warmth!'"

Although American troops are issued helmet liners by the military, those garments are made of synthetic materials which are not as warm as wool. Wool also has the added benefit of being naturally fire-resistant. Linda began getting the word out to knitters across the nation, inviting them to make wool helmet liners for the troops.

When health concerns prevented the Swinfords from continuing their work, they turned Operation Helmetliner over to Citizen Support for America's Military. "Citizen SAM" is a nonprofit organization offering several programs to support the Armed Forces community. To date, more than 240,000 wool helmet liners have been shipped to American troops through Citizen SAM. Shipping is paid through donations, since Citizen SAM receives no funding. Black is the preferred color for helmet liners, although dark brown and dark gray are also acceptable.

For more information about Citizen SAM and Operation Helmetliner, visit **www.citizensam.org** or call 309-693-9533.

The following are notes of appreciation from American service personnel who have received hand-knitted wool helmet liners.

> "It means a great deal to those of us serving that there are kind and generous people back home thinking about us. Your gifts will be heavily used and highly regarded."

> "Thank you for the wooly pulleys. All the troops stationed here (in Afghanistan) will appreciate them this winter. Please pass on my thanks to all the people who participated in this project."

Send your finished helmet liners along with yarn label indicating **100% wool** content to:

Citizen SAM
PO Box 10565
Peoria, Illinois 61612

www.citizensam.org
309-693-9533

Pattern Suggestions:

Helmet Liner
(page 20)

Scarf
(page 26)

Phillip's Wish

"Mom, is everybody warm?"

Phillip's Wish is a non-profit organization that began when a seven-year-old boy named Phillip Pruitt asked his mother a heartbreaking question.

Phillip and his mother, Cyndi Bunch, had been searching the streets of Fort Worth, Texas, looking for Phillip's father who suffered from mental illness. They were overwhelmed by the number of homeless people they saw. Unsuccessful at locating Phillip's father, they returned home. However, Phillip couldn't forget what he had seen.

He asked his mother if his father was warm, wherever he was. And then he asked, "Mom, is everybody warm?"

Cyndi sadly told him the truth, that not everyone was warm. It was the moment that changed the lives of mother and son.

They began collecting blankets to give to every homeless person they found. As of the end of 2008, with the help and support of other concerned individuals, organizations, and businesses, more than 75,000 blankets have been collected and distributed in the Fort Worth area. Other items donated include hundreds of hats, scarves, gloves, mittens, sleeping bags, toiletries, and thousands of toys.

What began as a child's wish for the comfort of others has spread to thousands of volunteers who support blanket drives in the area.

During each Christmas season, volunteers fill their private vehicles with loads of donated blankets, coats, and toiletries. As a caravan, they drive to an all but forgotten area of Forth Worth, where the homeless meet the volunteers with all the joy of children awaiting Santa's arrival. Witnesses to these events report their own joy in seeing homeless individuals assist one another in locating the items they need. The spirit of giving, it seems, is not limited to only those who already have plenty.

If you decide to create warm blankets or clothing for the homeless in your own community, be sure to visit **www.PhillipsWish.com** to read Cyndi's notes on approaching the homeless. Since a small number of those living on the streets can be aggressive, the safest way for you to help is to give your donations to the shelters and organizations who serve your local area. These agencies are often listed in regional phone books under Social Services, Welfare Organizations, and Human Services.

"With the worsening economy," Cyndi says, "there are more people in need of help than ever before."

To help the homeless living in the Fort Worth area, send your knit blankets and warm garments to:

Phillip's Wish
12188 Thicket Bend Dr.
Keller, Texas 76248

www.PhillipsWish.com

Pattern Suggestions:

Cuffed Hat
(page 17)

Scarf
(page 26)

Mittens
(page 27)

Mariner's Vest
(page 54)

Baby Blanket
(page 58)

Afghan
(page 60)

Bulky Sweater
(page 64)

Project Linus

Warm Hugs for Children in Need

The Project Linus Mission Statement

First, it is our mission to provide love, a sense of security, warmth and comfort to children who are seriously ill, traumatized, or otherwise in need through the gifts of new handmade blankets and afghans, lovingly created by volunteer "blanketeers."

Second, it is our mission to provide a rewarding and fun service opportunity for interested individuals and groups in local communities, for the benefit of children.

www.ProjectLinus.org

Pattern Suggestions:

Baby Blanket
(page 58)

Afghan
(page 60)

In late 1995, Karen Loucks read an article in Parade Magazine that touched her heart. The story highlighted a fragile little girl who had been undergoing intensive chemotherapy. The child stated that her security blanket helped her get through the treatments. The story inspired Karen to begin providing security blankets to Denver's Rocky Mountain Children's Center. This was the birth of Project Linus, an organization of volunteers who have created more than 3,000,000 blankets for children in need.

Today, Project Linus National Headquarters is located in Bloomington, Illinois. National President Carol Babbitt and Vice President Mary Balagna direct the activities of Project Linus chapters across the United States. With chapters in all 50 states, Project Linus continues to grow. Blankets are collected locally and distributed to children in hospitals, shelters, social service agencies, or anywhere a child might be in need of a big hug.

"I am extremely pleased by the outpouring of support Project Linus has enjoyed." states Babbitt. "The comfort brought to a child by a Project Linus security blanket should not be underestimated. Thanks to our many volunteers and our chapter coordinators, millions of children and their families have been given security at a time when they need it most. In addition, volunteers have an opportunity to use their talents and abilities in a most rewarding way."

Project Linus volunteers, also known as "blanketeers," provide new, handmade, washable blankets to be given as gifts to seriously ill and traumatized children, ages newborn to eighteen years. Depending on local chapter needs, Project Linus accepts blankets of all sizes. All styles of blankets are welcome, including quilts, tied comforters, fleece blankets, crocheted or knitted afghans, and receiving blankets in child-friendly colors. Blankets must be homemade, washable, free of pins, and come from smoke-free environments due to allergy concerns.

To learn more about this organization and locate a volunteer chapter in your area, visit **www.ProjectLinus.org**.

Santa Train
A Christmas Tradition Keeps Rolling Along

When Santa visits the coalfields of Virginia, Kentucky, and Tennessee, he travels the rails on his very own train!

At 110 miles in length, The Santa Claus Special is the world's largest Santa parade. On the Saturday before Thanksgiving, volunteers from the city of Kingsport, Tennessee join the railroad employees of CSX Transportation, Inc., the Kingsport Chamber of Commerce, and Food City to take fifteen tons of goodies, toys, and gifts to the people of the region. The train makes thirteen stops and travels through twenty-nine towns along the route from Pikeville, Kentucky to Kingsport, Tennessee.

The Santa Claus Special has been rolling annually since 1943, gaining popularity each year. Started as a way for area businesses to thank their patrons, the train now also accepts donations, including new clothes and new toys from individuals. In fact, financial gifts from the public have helped establish the Santa Train Scholarship for students who live along the train's route.

Hand-knit scarves, gloves, mittens, and hats are welcome gifts presented at each train stop. All sizes are needed, with special emphasis on items for children.

For more information about Santa Train or the Santa Train Scholarship, visit **www.kingsportchamber.org** and click on "Programs," or call 423-392-8800.

To contribute your knit items to be distributed from The Santa Claus Special, send them to:

Kingsport Area
Chamber of Commerce
Attn: Santa Train
151 East Main Street
Kingsport, TN 37660

www.kingsportchamber.org
423-392-8800

Pattern Suggestions:

Cuffed Hat
(page 17)

Hooded Scarf
(page 24)

Scarf
(page 26)

Mittens
(page 27)

Slippers
(page 30)

All I need is a Snuggle and a place to call home.
www.snugglesproject.org

For more information, visit:

www.snugglesproject.org

www.h4ha.org

Pattern Suggestion:

Animal's Blanket
(page 62)

Snuggles Project
Creating Comfort for Shelter Animals

Each year, millions of animals are given up to shelters where the pens and enclosures often provide little in the way of physical comfort or warmth.

For Rae French of Portland, Oregon, the president of 501(c)(3) nonprofit Hugs for Homeless Animals, knowledge of these living conditions prevented her from taking the homeless cats in her neighborhood to a local shelter. Instead, she fed and cared for each stray that came to her until 1996, when she started the Snuggles Project.

"Snuggles" are security blankets for homeless dogs and cats. These blankets provide physical and psychological comfort for shelter pets, giving them a softer alternative to resting on the floors of their pens.

Knitters will be happy to know that Snuggles are a wonderful way to use up leftover yarn. Snuggles must be machine washable, so volunteers should choose yarn accordingly. Yarn ends should be double-knotted and fastened off with long lengths that are woven through the work to prevent unraveling.

Suggested sizes for Snuggles are 14", 24", and 36" squares. These blankets are an excellent project for beginning knitters, because perfection isn't a requirement. The animals just need these expressions of love to be closely worked for maximum warmth and safety.

Snuggles should be donated directly to the participating shelters listed at **www.h4ha.org/shelters** under "Shelter Index." Before donating your blankets to a shelter that isn't listed in the directory, be sure they have the facilities to wash blankets.

"I am so very happy that the Snuggles Project has become so popular," says Rae French, "My heart is overjoyed each time someone donates a Snuggle to a homeless animal. I hope after you read this, you will want to help, too."

Warm Up America!

Because she wanted to help the homeless, Evie Rosen of Wausau, Wisconsin came up with an idea in 1991 that has eventually produced more than 250,000 afghans for people in need.

At the time, Evie was a yarn retailer. She asked customers, friends, and her local community to knit and crochet 7" x 9" sections to be joined into afghans. The concept, named "Warm Up America!," quickly became an overwhelming success. In 1995, Evie turned to the Craft Yarn Council of America, a non-profit association of yarn companies and publishers, for assistance. Warm Up America! soon became a national, grassroots program. It is now a 501(c)(3) tax exempt, charitable organization.

Volunteers for Warm Up America! continue to make knitted and crocheted afghan blankets, clothing, and accessories to help those in need. These items provide comfort to people who have lost their homes, fled abusive relationships, or who are being cared for in hospices, shelters, hospitals, and nursing homes. Many thousands of handmade items are distributed to various charities each year.

The 7" X 9" knitted or crocheted sections are joined into afghans that are a beautiful patchwork of many colors and textures, just as the participants and recipients represent the varied faces of America. There are two **Warm Up America! Blocks** for afghans on pages 69 and 70 to get you started on your mission to help Warm Up America!

To learn more about how you or your organization can get involved, visit **www.WarmUpAmerica.org**. You'll find tips on how to start a charity knitting group, getting children involved, and where to look in your area for agencies and organizations that need your afghans. Please note that Warm Up America! can only accept new afghans.

Because the Warm Up America! Foundation receives many individual knitted and crocheted sections, they encourage you to work locally whenever possible to complete and donate your afghans. However, if you cannot join the 7" x 9" sections into a blanket, you may send them to:

Warm Up America!
Foundation
469 Hospital Drive,
2nd Floor Suite E
Gastonia, NC 28054

www.WarmUpAmerica.org

Pattern Suggestion:

Warm Up America! Blocks
(pages 69 and 70)

Send your finished, **100% wool** garments and accessories to:

Warm Woolies
5572 E. Mansfield Avenue
Denver, CO 80237

www.warmwoolies.org

Warm Woolies

Creating Knitwear for Children in Need

In 2002, Kimberly Turnbow of Denver, Colorado learned that children in some of Russia's orphanages suffer a particular hardship. A good friend had just adopted two Russian children, and she shared with Kimberly how children in the coldest regions must dress in the warmest of clothes. However, the Russian caregivers are often challenged to keep their charges supplied with warm garments. Hearing this, Kimberly wanted to help as many children as she could.

She founded Warm Woolies, a non-profit organization whose volunteers knit wool clothing for poverty-stricken children who would otherwise suffer from cold. Their mission is to provide the very neediest children with wool sweaters, vests, socks, hats, and mittens.

Since the organization's beginnings, Warm Woolies volunteers have supplied knit items to children in Russia, Kazakhstan, Mongolia, Afghanistan, and China. They also provide warm garments to children on the Rosebud and Pine Ridge Reservations of South Dakota, and to other tribal communities throughout the northern United States. In 2008, Warm Woolies distributed more than 12,000 hand-knit items.

"We have guidelines to ensure that the garments will truly be of use to the children," says Kimberly. "The primary rule is that only wool yarn is used, because animal hair fibers are the warmest. Bulky or double worsted weight wool yarn, closely worked, is best. Finer wool yarns are only okay for the smallest of items. Also, a garment that is on the long side is always better than one that is too short, and sweaters must close securely all the way down. These children are newborn to sixteen years of age, so if your garment ends up a little large or small, it doesn't matter; there is a child who can wear it. If you only have acrylic yarn available to you, please use it to make large baby blankets, the warmer the better.

"We are excited about the growing number of volunteers of every skill level who help these children," Kimberly says. "Everyone who can knit or crochet is invited to send their handmade items. There are still many more children who need warm clothes."

If you can include 50 cents per item when you mail your finished pieces, it will help Warm Woolies cover shipping costs. For complete donation guidelines and information on current needs and goals, visit **www.warmwoolies.org**.

Helping at Home

Correctional Facilities

In correctional facilities across America, men and women are making productive use of their time served by knitting and crocheting. The blankets, toys, and garments they create give them a much-needed creative outlet—yet these skills don't just benefit the crafter. Depending on the programs in each facility, the handmade items produced are often donated directly to the local community, with items going to homeless shelters and children in need. Some of the incarcerated men and women choose to create gifts for their own children.

If you've been wondering what to do with all that yarn you never quite got around to using, consider donating it to your local correctional facility or nearby prison ministry. Because the yarn is made into useful items for the community, you'll be giving a gift twice over.

There are several ways to find out which local institutions are participating in inmate knitting and crochet programs. You can search the Internet for prison ministries and correctional facility knitting in your area. You can also contact the offices of area churches, temples, tabernacles, and social services agencies to learn if they participate in prison outreach through knitting.

If there aren't any facilities accepting yarn for prison programs in your county, parish, or state, visit interweaveknits.com for their list of facilities. Since these programs may have specific guidelines that are subject to change, it's a good idea to contact the listed organizations directly before shipping your yarn or other knitting supplies.

Hats for Chemotherapy Patients

As a knitter, you know that if a friend or family member is losing their hair due to medical treatment, you'll make that loved one a hat of the softest yarn you can find. You also know that he or she will enjoy your gift for two reasons: It helps the wearer feel more comfortable with their changing appearance, and it shows how much you care.

Unfortunately, not everyone undergoing chemotherapy will have the benefit of knowing someone who knits. That's why hospitals and outpatient clinics in your community want your donations of soft, washable, hand-knit hats and caps for their patients. A little research by phone or online will help you find one of these medical facilities in your area. There are also several charitable organizations that work regionally to gather and distribute hats. You can locate a number of these through Internet searches for the words "chemo caps" or "head huggers."

When you consider what kind of yarn to use, remember that a natural yarn like cotton is preferable during the warm months of the year or when the hat or cap will be worn indoors. Chemotherapy patients also prefer a cap pattern that offers good coverage of the sides and back of the head, such as the **Hug Cap** (pattern on page 22). It can be made to fit anyone from a small child to a large adult.

Helping at Home

Nursing Homes and Assisted Care Communities

When health concerns make it necessary for someone to move to a nursing home or assisted care community, the sudden lifestyle change can be disorienting and frightening. A gesture of caring, such as the gift of a knitted lap robe, afghan, or slippers, can be a source of comfort to someone experiencing a loss of independence. Not only is such a gift practical, it is daily proof to the recipient that he or she has not been forgotten.

When making an **Afghan** (pattern on page 60) or lap robe for someone with a disability, remember to use washable yarn that can withstand the heat of a dryer. Fringe, tassels, or an openwork pattern should be avoided since they can become tangled underfoot or caught in the mechanisms of a wheelchair.

Lap robes to be used by someone in a wheelchair are usually rectangular in shape. Finished sizes should be determined according to the size of the recipient. For example, a lap robe about 28" x 36" may be sufficient for a slender person of small to medium height, while a larger person may need a lap robe measuring 36" x 48" or more. **The Warm Up America! Blocks** (patterns on pages 69 and 70) can be used to create lap robes of varying sizes.

A pair of handknitted **Slippers** (pattern on page 30) is a thoughtful gift for someone who is confined to a bed or wheelchair. Keep in mind that knitted slippers may not provide enough traction for safety on the polished floors of care facilities. Ambulatory persons and individuals who can transfer themselves from bed to wheelchair will need shoes that provide more stability.

It will be helpful to the staff of the nursing home if you add a tag of white fabric to the back of the lap robe or afghan and the inside top of both slippers. Be sure to securely hem and sew all edges of the tag to the finished project. A tag makes it possible for you or a member of the care staff to write the recipient's name on their handknit items right away. Otherwise, your gifts may remain unused until a staff member finds the time to print and sew a tag.

Consult your phone directory to locate assisted-living centers and nursing homes in your community that accept handmade afghans, lap robes, or slippers on behalf of their clients.

cuffed hat

Size	Head Circumference		Finished Measurement	
Toddler	16"	(40.5 cm)	14"	(35.5 cm)
Child	18"	(45.5 cm)	15¼"	(38.5 cm)
Woman	20"	(51 cm)	17½"	(44.5 cm)
Man	22"	(56 cm)	20"	(51 cm)

Size Note: Instructions are written for Toddler size with size for Children, Women, and Men in the set of braces { }. Instructions will be easier to read if you circle all the numbers pertaining to your size. If only one number is given, it applies to all sizes.

MATERIALS

Medium Weight Yarn
[3.5 ounces, 220 yards
(100 grams, 201 meters) per hank]:
 1 hank
Straight knitting needles, size 6 (4 mm)
 or size needed for gauge
Yarn needle

GAUGE: In Stockinette Stitch,
 17 sts and 23 rows = 4" (10 cm)

CUFF

Cast on 62{67-77-87} sts **loosely**.

Row 1: K2, (P3, K2) across.

Row 2: P2, (K3, P2) across.

Repeat Rows 1 and 2 until Cuff measures approximately 1½{2½-3-3}"/4{6.5-7.5-7.5} cm from cast on edge, ending by working Row 2.

BODY

When instructed to slip a stitch, always slip as if to **purl** with yarn held loosely to **wrong** side.

Row 1 (Right side)**:** P2, (K1, slip 1, K1, P2) across.

Row 2: K2, (P3, K2) across.

Repeat Rows 1 and 2 for pattern until piece measures approximately 5{6½-9-9}"/12.5{16.5-23-23} cm from cast on edge, ending by working Row 1.

Instructions continued on page 18.

TOP SHAPING
SIZES FOR TODDLER & CHILD ONLY

Row 1 (Decrease row): K2, ★ P3, K2 tog **(Fig. 9, page 75)**; repeat from ★ across: 50{54} sts.

Row 2: ★ P1, K1, slip 1, K1; repeat from ★ across to last 2 sts, P2.

Row 3 (Decrease row): K2, ★ P1, P2 tog **(Fig. 12, page 76)**, K1; repeat from ★ across: 38{41} sts.

Row 4: ★ P1, slip 1, K1; repeat from ★ across to last 2 sts, P2.

Row 5 (Decrease row): K2, ★ SSP **(Fig. 14, page 76)**, K1; repeat from ★ across: 26{28} sts.

Row 6: ★ P1, K1; repeat from ★ across to last 2 sts, P2.

Row 7 (Decrease row): P2 tog across: 13{14} sts.

Row 8: Knit across.

SIZES FOR WOMAN & MAN ONLY

Row 1 (Decrease row): K2, ★ P3, K2 tog **(Fig. 9, page 75)**; repeat from ★ across: {62-70} sts.

Row 2: ★ P1, K1, slip 1, K1; repeat from ★ across to last 2 sts, P2.

Row 3: K2, ★ P3, K1; repeat from ★ across.

Row 4 (Decrease row): ★ P1, K2 tog, K1; repeat from ★ across to last 2 sts, P2: {47-53} sts.

Row 5: K2, ★ P2, K1; repeat from ★ across.

Row 6: ★ P1, slip 1, K1; repeat from ★ across to last 2 sts, P2.

Row 7 (Decrease row): K2, ★ SSP **(Fig. 14, page 76)**, K1; repeat from ★ across: {32-36} sts.

Row 8: ★ P1, slip 1; repeat from ★ across to last 2 sts, P2.

Row 9: K2, ★ P1, K1; repeat from ★ across.

Row 10 (Decrease row): K2 tog across: {16-18} sts.

Row 11: Purl across.

ALL SIZES

Cut yarn leaving a long length for sewing.

Thread yarn needle with end and slip remaining sts onto yarn needle; gather tightly to close and secure end. Weave seam reversing seam on Cuff so seam won't show when it's turned up **(Fig. 16, page 77)**.

Note: When sending 100% wool Hats to Citizen SAM, be sure to include the yarn label. Acrylic Hats can be sent to other charities.

Design by Cathy Hardy.

helmet liner

This hat, also known as a face mask, can be worn by the military under their helmets or by anyone in a cold climate for extra warmth and protection from the wind.

Adult Size	Head Circumference	Finished Measurement
Small	20" (51 cm)	18" (45.5 cm)
Medium	22" (56 cm)	20" (51 cm)

Size Note: Instructions are written for size Small with size Medium in braces { }. Instructions will be easier to read if you circle all the numbers pertaining to your size. If only one number is given, it applies to both sizes.

MATERIALS
Medium Weight Yarn (4)
[5 ounces, 260 yards
(141 grams, 238 meters) per skein]:
  1 skein
Knitting needles, size 6 (4 mm) **or** size needed for gauge *(see needle note below)*
Yarn needle

Needle Note: This Helmet is worked in the round. You will need one 16" (40.5 cm) circular needle for the Lower Section and the Eye Opening. The Top Shaping can be worked with double pointed needles *(see Double Pointed Needles, page 72)* or a second circular needle *(see Circular Knitting, pages 72 and 73)*. Use whichever method you prefer.

GAUGE: In Stockinette Stitch,
   17 sts and 23 rows = 4" (10 cm)

Gauge is very important for fit. Helmet Liner must fit snugly and not obstruct the wearer's vision.

LOWER SECTION
Cast on 84{94} sts **loosely**.

Note: The yarn end indicates the beginning of the round.

Work in K1, P1 ribbing until piece measures approximately 6{7}"/15{18} cm from cast on edge.

EYE OPENING
Work in established ribbing throughout.

Rnd 1: Work across 24{27} sts, bind off next 36{40} sts **loosely**, work across: 48{54} sts.

Rnd 2: Work across to bound off sts; **turn**, add on 36{40} sts **loosely** *(Figs. 7a & b, page 75)*; **turn**, work across: 84{94} sts.

Work even until piece measures approximately 10{12}"/25.5{30.5} cm from cast on edge.

TOP SHAPING
SIZE MEDIUM ONLY
Rnd 1 (Decrease row)**:** ★ K1, (P1, K1) 7 times, P3 tog *(Fig. 13, page 76)*; repeat from ★ around to last 4 sts, (K1, P1) twice: 84 sts.

Rnds 2 and 3: Work around.

BOTH SIZES

Change to double pointed needles placing a multiple of 12 sts on each needle **or** use a second circular needle for the first 36 sts.

Rnd 1{4} (Decrease rnd): ★ K1, (P1, K1) 4 times, P3 tog *(Fig. 13, page 76)*; repeat from ★ around: 70 sts.

Rnds 2{5} and 3{6}: Work around.

Rnd 4{7} (Decrease rnd): ★ K1, (P1, K1) 3 times, P3 tog; repeat from ★ around: 56 sts.

Rnds 5{8} and 6{9}: Work around.

Rnd 7{10} (Decrease rnd): ★ K1, (P1, K1) twice, P3 tog; repeat from ★ around: 42 sts.

Rnds 8{11} and 9{12}: Work around.

Rnd 10{13} (Decrease rnd): ★ K1, P1, K1, P3 tog; repeat from ★ around: 28 sts.

Rnds 11{14} and 12{15}: Work around.

Rnd 13{16} (Decrease rnd): (K1, P3 tog) around: 14 sts.

Rnd 14{17}: Work around.

Cut yarn leaving a long length for sewing.

Thread yarn needle with end and slip remaining sts onto yarn needle; gather tightly to close and secure end.

Note: When sending 100% wool Helmet Liners to Citizen SAM, be sure to include the yarn label. Acrylic Helmet Liners can be sent to Christmas at Sea.

Design by Edna Lipner.

hug cap

Size	Head Circumference		Finished Measurement	
Children				
Small	16¹/₂"	(42 cm)	14¹/₂"	(37 cm)
Medium	18"	(45.5 cm)	16"	(40.5 cm)
Large	19¹/₂"	(49.5 cm)	17¹/₂"	(44.5 cm)
Adult				
Small	21"	(53.5 cm)	19"	(48.5 cm)
Medium	22¹/₂"	(57 cm)	21"	(53.5 cm)
Large	24"	(61 cm)	22¹/₂"	(57 cm)

Size Note: Instructions are written with sizes for Children in the first set of braces { } and with sizes for Adults in the second set of braces. Instructions will be easier to read if you circle all the numbers pertaining to your size. If only one number is given, it applies to all sizes.

MATERIALS

Medium Weight Yarn 🔵(4)
[3.5 ounces, 178 yards
(100 grams, 163 meters) per skein]:
  {1-1-1}{1-1-2} skein(s)
Knitting needles, size 6 (4 mm) **or** size needed for gauge *(see needle note)*
Yarn needle

Yarn Note: A soft cotton or cotton blend yarn will make a cap that will be comfortable and cooler to wear, as this cap is for looks not for warmth.

Needle Note: This Cap is worked in the round with either double pointed needles *(see Double Pointed Needles, page 72)*, or circular needles. Begin the larger sizes with one 16" (40.5 cm) circular needle and the smallest size with two. Change to two circular needles on the larger sizes when beginning the Top Shaping *(see Circular Knitting, pages 72 and 73)*. Use whichever method you prefer.

GAUGE: In Stockinette Stitch,
          20 sts and 27 rows = 4" (10 cm)

BODY

Cast on {72-80-88}{96-104-112} sts **loosely**.

Note: The yarn end indicates the beginning of the round.

Rnds 1-5: Knit around.

Rnd 6: (K3, P5) around.

Rnds 7-9: ★ K3, P2, K1, P2; repeat from ★ around.

Rnds 10-12: (K3, P5) around.

Repeat Rnds 7-12, {2-3-3}{4-4-5} times; then repeat Rnds 7-10 once **more**.

TOP SHAPING

Rnd 1: ★ K3, P2 tog *(Fig. 12, page 76)*, P3; repeat from ★ around: {63-70-77}{84-91-98} sts.

Rnd 2: (K3, P4) around.

Rnd 3: ★ K3, P1, K1, P2; repeat from ★ around.

Rnd 4: ★ K3, P1, K1, P2 tog; repeat from ★ around: {54-60-66} {72-78-84} sts.

Rnd 5: ★ K3, P1, K1, P1; repeat from ★ around.

Rnd 6: (K3, P3) around.

Rnd 7: ★ K3, P2 tog, P1; repeat from ★ around: {45-50-55}{60-65-70} sts.

Rnds 8 and 9: (K3, P2) around.

Rnd 10: ★ K1, K2 tog *(Fig. 9, page 75)*, P2; repeat from ★ around: {36-40-44}{48-52-56} sts.

CHILDREN SIZES ONLY
Rnd 11: (K2 tog, P2 tog) around: {18-20-22} sts.

ADULT SIZES ONLY
Rnds 11 and 12: (K2, P2) around.

Rnd 13: (K2, P2 tog) around: {36-39-42} sts.

Rnd 14: (K2 tog, P1) around: {24-26-28} sts.

ALL SIZES
Cut yarn leaving a long length for sewing.

Thread yarn needle with end and slip remaining sts onto yarn needle; gather tightly to close and secure end.

Design by Cathy Hardy.

hooded scarf

Finished Measurement:
  Hood - 8" high x 18" wide (20.5 cm x 45.5 cm)
  Attached Scarf - 6" wide x 21" long
    (15 cm x 53.5 cm)

MATERIALS
  Medium Weight Yarn 〔4〕
  [5 ounces, 256 yards
  (142 grams, 234 meters) per skein]:
    Main Color (Blue) - 2 skeins
  [4 ounces, 204 yards
  (113 grams, 187 meters) per skein]:
    Contrasting Color (Variegated) - 1 skein
  Straight knitting needles, size 8 (5 mm)
    or size needed for gauge
  Yarn needle

GAUGE: In Stockinette Stitch,
        17 sts and 23 rows = 4" (10 cm)

RIGHT SCARF
With Main Color, cast on 25 sts **loosely**.

Rows 1-7: K1, (P1, K1) across (Seed Stitch).

Rows 8-11: With Contrasting Color, knit across (Garter Stitch stripe).

Rows 12-25: With Main Color, K1, (P1, K1) across.

Repeat Rows 8-25 for pattern until Right Scarf measures approximately 21" (53.5 cm) from cast on edge, ending by working Row 25.

HOOD
Row 1: Bind off 6 sts **loosely** in pattern, K2, knit into the front **and** into the back of each st across to last 3 sts **(Figs. 8a & b, page 75)**, K3: 32 sts.

Beginning with a **purl** row, work in Stockinette Stitch (purl one row, knit one row) until Hood measures approximately 16" (40.5 cm), ending by working a **purl** row.

LEFT SCARF
Row 1: Add on 6 sts **loosely** **(Figs. 7a & b, page 75)**, K1, (P1, K1) 4 times, K2 tog across to last 3 sts **(Fig. 9, page 75)**, K3: 25 sts.

Beginning with Row 12, work in same pattern as Right Scarf until Left Scarf measures same as Right Scarf, ending by working Row 18.

Bind off all sts **loosely** in pattern.

FRONT RIBBING
With **right** side facing, pick up 77 sts evenly spaced along Hood edge, between bound off and added on sts **(Fig. 15b, page 76)**.

Row 1: K1, (P1, K1) across.

Row 2: P1, (K1, P1) across.

Repeat Rows 1 and 2 until ribbing measures approximately 1½" (4 cm).

Bind off all sts **loosely** in ribbing.

Sew edges of Front Ribbing to Scarf.

Fold Hood in half and weave Hood seam from center to beginning of Scarf *(Fig. 16, page 77)*.

Add pom-pom to top of Hood *(Figs. 18a-c, page 78)*.

Design by Cathy Hardy.

scarf

●□□□ BEGINNER

Finished Size: 12" x 42"
  (30.5 cm x 106.5 cm)

MATERIALS

Medium Weight Yarn **④** MEDIUM
[3.52 ounces, 166 yards
(100 grams, 152 meters) per skein]:
  Main Color (Taupe) - 2 skeins
  Color A (Green) - 1 skein
  Color B (Grey) - 1 skein
Straight knitting needles, size 8
  (5 mm) **or** size needed for gauge

GAUGE: In pattern,
      24 sts and 24 rows = 4" (10 cm)

Measure gauge while piece is relaxed.

BODY

With Main Color, cast on 72 sts **loosely**.

Rows 1-6: (K1, P1) across.

Rows 7-12: (P1, K1) across.

Repeat Rows 1-12 for pattern until Scarf
measures approximately 42" (106.5 cm)
from cast on edge working in the
following stripe sequence: 6 rows Color A,
12 rows Main Color, ★ 6 rows Color B,
12 rows Main Color, 6 rows Color A,
12 rows Main Color; repeat from ★ for
sequence.

Bind off all sts **loosely** in ribbing.

mittens

◼◼◻◻ EASY +

Size	Hand Circumference	
Children		
Small	5"	(12.5 cm)
Medium	5½"	(14 cm)
Large	6"	(15 cm)
Women		
Small	6½"	(16.5 cm)
Medium	7"	(18 cm)
Large	7½"	(19 cm)
Men		
Small	8"	(20.5 cm)
Medium	8½"	(21.5 cm)
Large	9"	(23 cm)

Size Note: Instructions are written with sizes for Children in the first set of braces { }, with sizes for Women in the second set of braces and with sizes for Men in the third set of braces. Instructions will be easier to read if you circle all the numbers pertaining to your size. If only one number is given, it applies to all sizes.

Hand circumference should be measured around the widest part of the palm just above thumb.

MATERIALS
Worsted Weight Yarn
Solid **[7 ounces, 364 yards (198 grams, 333 meters) per skein] or** Variegated **[5 ounces, 244 yards (141 grams, 223 meters) per skein]:**
1 skein
Straight knitting needles, sizes 5 (3.75 mm) **and** 7 (4.5 mm) **or** sizes needed for gauge
Markers
Stitch holders - 2
Yarn needle

GAUGE: With larger size needles, in Stockinette Stitch, 20 sts = 4" (10 cm)

Instructions begin on page 28.

CUFF

Using smaller size needles, cast on {23-25-27}{29-31-33}{35-37-39} sts **loosely**.

Row 1: P1, (K1, P1) across.

Row 2 (Right side): K1, (P1, K1) across.

Repeat Rows 1 and 2 until piece measures approximately {2-2$\frac{1}{2}$-2$\frac{1}{2}$}{2$\frac{3}{4}$-3-3}{3$\frac{1}{4}$-3$\frac{1}{4}$-3$\frac{1}{2}$}"/{5-6.5-6.5}{7-7.5-7.5}{8.5-8.5-9} cm from cast on edge, ending by working Row 1.

BODY

Change to larger size needles.

Increases are made by knitting into the front **and** into the back of the next st **(Figs. 8a & b, page 75)**.

Row 1: Knit across increasing {5-5-5}{5-7-7}{7-9-9} sts evenly spaced: {28-30-32}{34-38-40}{42-46-48} sts.

Row 2: Purl across.

Men's Sizes Only - Rows 3 and 4: Work across in Stockinette Stitch.

SHAPING

Row 1: Knit {13-14-15}{16-18-19}{20-22-23} sts, place marker **(see Markers, page 72)**, increase twice, place marker, knit across: {30-32-34}{36-40-42}{44-48-50} sts.

Row 2: Purl across.

Row 3: Knit to marker, increase, knit to within one st of marker, increase, knit across: {32-34-36}{38-42-44}{46-50-52} sts.

Repeat Rows 2 and 3, {1-2-2}{3-3-4}{4-5-5} time(s): {34-38-40}{44-48-52}{54-60-62} sts.

Work even in Stockinette Stitch until piece measures approximately {3$\frac{1}{4}$-4-4}{4$\frac{3}{4}$-5-5$\frac{1}{4}$}{5$\frac{3}{4}$-6-6$\frac{1}{4}$}"/{8.5-10-10}{12-12.5-13.5}{14.5-15-16} cm from cast on edge, ending by working a **purl** row.

THUMB

Row 1: Knit to marker and slip these {13-14-15}{16-18-19}{20-22-23} sts onto st holder, add on one st **(Figs. 7a & b, page 75)**; knit to marker, remove marker, **turn**; add on one st, slip remaining sts onto second st holder: {10-12-12}{14-14-16}{16-18-18} sts.

Work even until Thumb measures approximately {1$\frac{1}{4}$-1$\frac{1}{2}$-1$\frac{3}{4}$}{2-2$\frac{1}{4}$-2$\frac{1}{2}$}{2$\frac{1}{2}$-2$\frac{3}{4}$-2$\frac{3}{4}$}"/{3-4-4.5}{5-5.5-6.5}{6.5-7-7} cm, ending by working a **purl** row.

Next Row: K2 tog across: {5-6-6}{7-7-8}{8-9-9} sts.

Cut yarn leaving a long length for sewing.

Thread yarn needle with end and slip remaining sts onto yarn needle; gather tightly to close and secure end. Weave seam **(Fig. 16, page 77)**.

HAND

With **right** side facing, slip sts from first st holder onto needle; pick up a st in each of 2 added on sts at base of Thumb **(Fig. 15b, page 76)**; slip sts from second st holder onto empty needle and knit across: {28-30-32}{34-38-40}{42-46-48} sts.

Work even until piece measures approximately {4³/₄-6-6}{7-7¹/₂-7³/₄} {8¹/₂-8³/₄-9¹/₄}"/{12-15-15} {18-19-19.5}{21.5-22-23.5} cm from cast on edge, ending by working a **knit** row.

Next Row: Purl {14-15-16} {17-19-20}{21-23-24} sts, place marker, purl across.

SHAPING
Row 1: K2, [slip 1 as if to **knit**, K1, PSSO *(Fig. 11, page 75)*], knit to within 3 sts of marker, K2 tog *(Fig. 9, page 75)*, K2, slip 1 as if to **knit**, K1, PSSO, knit across to last 4 sts, K2 tog, K2: {24-26-28}{30-34-36} {38-42-44} sts.

Row 2: Purl across.

Repeat Rows 1 and 2, {1-2-3}{3-4-5}{5-5-5} time(s): {20-18-16}{18-18-16} {18-22-24} sts.

Next Row: K2 tog across: {10-9-8}{9-9-8}{9-11-12} sts.

Cut yarn leaving a long length for sewing.

Thread yarn needle with end and slip remaining sts onto yarn needle; gather tightly to close and secure end. Weave seam.

Repeat for second Mitten.

Design by Mary Lamb Becker.

Size	Sole Length	
Small	7"	(18 cm)
Medium	8½"	(21.5 cm)
Large	10"	(25.5 cm)

MATERIALS

Medium Weight Yarn **(4)**
[7 ounces, 364 yards
(198 grams, 333 meters) per skein]:
   1 skein
Straight knitting needles, size 10 (6 mm) **or**
   size needed for gauge
Yarn needle

Entire Slipper is worked holding two strands of yarn together.

GAUGE: In Garter Stitch,
   14 sts and 24 rows = 4" (10 cm)

BODY

Cast on 39 sts **loosely**.

Row 1: K 14, P1, K9, P1, K 14.

Row 2 (Right side)**:** Knit across.

Repeat Rows 1 and 2 for pattern until piece measures approximately 4" (10 cm) for Small, 5½" (14 cm) for Medium, or 7" (18 cm) for Large, ending by working Row 2.

TOE

Row 1: Bind off 5 sts, K8, P1, K9, P1, K 14: 34 sts.

Row 2: Bind off 5 sts, knit across: 29 sts.

Row 3: K1, (P1, K1) across.

Row 4: P1, (K1, P1) across.

Rows 5-14: Repeat Rows 3 and 4, 5 times.

FINISHING

Cut yarn leaving a long length for sewing.

Thread yarn needle with end and slip remaining sts onto yarn needle. Fold the Slipper in half lengthwise with **right** sides together. Pull yarn tightly to close and catch the first and last stitches together to secure. Sew the instep from the toe to the top of the bound off stitches, catching one stitch from each side and being careful to match rows.

Sew the back seam from the top edge to the Stockinette Stitch lines and secure. Weave the needle through each of the remaining 9 sts; pull very tightly to close and secure.

Design by Evie Rosen.

thick SOCKS

Children Size	Finished Foot Circumference	
Small	5"	(12.5 cm)
Medium	6"	(15 cm)
Large	6³/₄"	(17 cm)
X-Large	7¹/₂"	(19 cm)

Size Note: Instructions are written for size Small with sizes Medium, Large, and X-Large in braces { }. Instructions will be easier to read if you circle all the numbers pertaining to your child's size. If only one number is given, it applies to all sizes.

MATERIALS
Medium Weight Yarn 🧶 **4**
[3.5 ounces, 220 yards
(100 grams, 201 meters) per hank]:
  1 hank
Two 16" (40.5 cm) Circular knitting needles,
  size 5 (3.75 mm) **or** size needed for gauge
Yarn needle

GAUGE: In Stockinette Stitch,
        19 sts = 4" (10 cm)

CUFF
Cast on 24{28-32-36} sts on one circular needle.

Slip the last 12{14-16-18} sts onto the second circular needle, placing them at the center of the cable *(Figs. 2b-d, page 73)*.

Note: The yarn end indicates the beginning of the round.

Work in K1, P1 ribbing for
1{1-1¹/₂-2}"/2.5{2.5-4-5} cm.

LEG
When instructed to slip a stitch, always slip as if to **purl** with yarn held loosely to **wrong** side.

Rnd 1: ★ Slip 1, K1; repeat from ★ around.

Rnd 2: Knit around.

Repeat Rnds 1 and 2 until Sock measures approximately 3¹/₂{4¹/₂-5¹/₂-6}"/9{11.5-14-15} cm from cast on edge, ending by working Rnd 2.

HEEL FLAP
Begin working in rows on the first needle only. The stitches on the second needle won't be used until the Gusset. The following pattern will make the Heel dense and will help prevent it from wearing out.

Row 1: ★ Slip 1, K1; repeat from ★ across.

Row 2: ★ Slip 1, P1; repeat from ★ across.

Repeat Rows 1 and 2, 4{5-5-6} times.

TURN HEEL
Begin working in short rows as follows:

Row 1: Slip 1, K6{7-8-9}, SSK *(Figs. 10a-c, page 75)*, K1, leave remaining 2{3-4-5} sts unworked; **turn**.

Row 2: Slip 1, P3, P2 tog *(Fig. 12, page 76)*, P1, leave remaining 2{3-4-5} sts unworked; turn.

Row 3: Slip 1, K4, SSK, K1; turn.

Row 4: Slip 1, P5, P2 tog, P1; turn.

SIZE MEDIUM ONLY
Row 5: Slip 1, K6, SSK.

Row 6: Slip 1, P6, P2 tog: 8 sts.

Instructions continued on page 37.

socks

●●●◻ INTERMEDIATE

Adult Size	Finished Foot Circumference	
Small	8"	(20.5 cm)
Medium	9"	(23 cm)
Large	10¼"	(26 cm)

Size Note: Instructions are written for size Small with sizes Medium and Large in braces { }. Instructions will be easier to read if you circle all the numbers pertaining to your size. If only one number is given, it applies to all sizes.

MATERIALS

Super Fine Weight Self Striping Yarn
[3.5 ounces, 425 yards
(100 grams, 388 meters) per skein]: 1 skein
Set of 5 double pointed knitting needles,
   sizes 3 (3.25 mm) **and** 4 (3.5 mm) **or** sizes
   needed for gauge
Stitch holders - 2
Split-ring marker
Tapestry needle

Yarn Note: Since a tight gauge is desirable for warmth, a fine/sport weight yarn can be substituted as long as gauge is obtained.

GAUGE: With smaller size needles,
   in Stockinette Stitch,
   28 sts and 36 rnds = 4" (10 cm)

LEG

With larger size needle, cast on 56{64-72} sts.

Slip 14{16-18} sts onto each of 4 double pointed needles *(Fig. 1, page 72)*.

Note: The yarn end indicates the beginning of the round.

Rnd 1: ★ K3, P1, (K1, P1) twice; repeat from ★ around.

Rnd 2: ★ K3, P2, K1, P2; repeat from ★ around.

Repeat Rnds 1 and 2 until Leg measures approximately 2{2½-3}"/5{6.5-7.5} cm from cast on edge.

Change to smaller size needles.

Continue to repeat Rnds 1 and 2 for pattern until Leg measures approximately 6{7-8}"/15{18-20.5} cm from cast on edge **or** 1" (2.5 cm) less than desired length.

Knit each round (Stockinette Stitch) for 1" (2.5 cm).

HEEL FLAP

Dividing Stitches: Knit across first needle; slip sts from the next 2 needles onto 2 separate st holders for Instep to be worked later; **turn.**

Note: The following pattern will make the Heel dense and will help prevent it from wearing out. Work Row 1 across both needles onto one needle. The Heel Flap will be worked back and forth across these 28{32-36} sts.

When instructed to slip a stitch, always slip as if to **purl** with yarn held to **wrong** side.

Row 1: ★ Slip 1, P1; repeat from ★ across.

Row 2: ★ Slip 1, K1; repeat from ★ across.

Repeat Rows 1 and 2, 13{15-17} times; then repeat Row 1 once **more**.

TURN HEEL

Begin working in short rows as follows:

Row 1: Slip 1, K 16{20-24}, SSK *(Figs. 10a-c, page 75)*, K1, leave remaining 8 sts unworked; **turn**.

Instructions continued on page 36.

socks

Continued from page 35.

Row 2: Slip 1, P 7{11-15}, P2 tog *(Fig. 12, page 76)*, P1, leave remaining 8 sts unworked; turn.

Row 3: Slip 1, K 8{12-16}, SSK, K1; turn.

Row 4: Slip 1, P 9{13-17}, P2 tog, P1; turn.

Rows 5-10: Repeat Rows 3 and 4, 3 times adding one st before decrease: 18{22-26} sts.

GUSSET

The remainder of the sock will be worked in rounds.

Slip the Instep sts from the st holders onto 2 double pointed needles, 14{16-18} sts each.

FOUNDATION ROUND

With **right** side of Heel facing, using an empty double pointed needle and continuing with the working yarn, knit 9{11-13} of the Heel sts. Place a split-ring marker around the next st to indicate the beginning of the round *(see Markers, page 72)*. Using an empty double pointed needle (this will be needle 1), knit across the remaining 9{11-13} Heel sts. With the same needle, pick up 14{16-18} sts along the side of the Heel Flap *(Fig. 15a, page 76)* and one st in the corner.
With separate needles, knit across the Instep sts (needles 2 and 3).
With an empty needle, pick up one st in the corner and 14{16-18} sts along the side of the Heel Flap. With the same needle, knit 9{11-13} Heel sts.

Stitch count is 24{28-32} sts on the first needle, 14{16-18} sts each on the second and third needles, and 24{28-32} sts on fourth needle for a total of 76{88-100} sts.

GUSSET DECREASES

Rnd 1 (Decrease rnd)**:** Knit across to the last 3 sts on first needle, K2 tog *(Fig. 9, page 75)*, K1; knit across the second and third needles; on fourth needle, K1, SSK, knit across: 74{86-98} sts.

Rnd 2: Knit around.

Repeat Rnds 1 and 2, 9{11-13} times: 56{64-72} sts, 14{16-18} sts on each needle.

FOOT

Work even knitting each round until Foot measures approximately 7$\frac{1}{2}${8$\frac{1}{2}$-9}"/19{21.5-23} cm from back of Heel or 1$\frac{3}{4}${1$\frac{3}{4}$-2$\frac{1}{4}$}"/4.5{4.5-5.5} cm less than total desired Foot length from back of Heel to Toe.

TOE

Rnd 1 (Decrease rnd)**:** Knit across first needle to last 3 sts, K2 tog, K1; on second needle, K1, SSK, knit across; on third needle, knit across to last 3 sts, K2 tog, K1; on fourth needle, K1, SSK, knit across: 4 sts decreased, 52{60-68} sts.

Rnd 2: Knit around.

Repeat Rnds 1 and 2, 7{7-9} times: 24{32-32} sts, 6{8-8} sts on each needle.

Using the fourth needle, knit across the sts on the first needle; cut yarn leaving a long end.

Slip the sts from the third needle onto the second needle, so there are 12{16-16} sts on each needle.

Graft remaining stitches together *(Figs. 17a & b, page 77)*.

Repeat for second Sock.

Design by Cathy Hardy.

thick socks

Continued from page 33.

SIZE LARGE ONLY
Row 5: Slip 1, K6, SSK, K1.

Row 6: Slip 1, P7, P2 tog, P1: 10 sts.

SIZE X-LARGE ONLY
Row 5: Slip 1, K6, SSK, K1; turn.

Row 6: Slip 1, P7, P2 tog, P1; turn.

Row 7: Slip 1, K8, SSK.

Row 8: Slip 1, P8, P2 tog: 10 sts.

GUSSET
Begin working with two circular needles in the round.

Rnd 1: Still using first needle, knit across the Heel sts, pick up 5{6-6-7} sts working in the end of rows along side of Heel Flap *(Fig. 15a, page 76)*; with the second needle, (slip 1, K1) across the Leg.

Rnd 2: Using first needle, pick up 5{6-6-7} sts in the end of rows along second side of Heel Flap, knit to end of needle; knit across second needle: 18{20-22-24} sts on the first needle and 12{14-16-18} sts on the second needle.

Rnd 3: K1, SSK, knit across first needle to last 3 sts, K2 tog *(Fig. 9, page 75)*, K1; (slip 1, K1) across second needle: 16{18-20-22} sts on first needle.

Rnd 4: Knit around.

Repeat Rnds 3 and 4 twice: 12{14-16-18} sts on **each** needle.

FOOT
Rnd 1: Knit across first needle; (slip 1, K1) across second needle.

Rnd 2: Knit around.

Repeat Rnds 1 and 2 until Foot measures approximately 4{4-4³/₄-6³/₄}"/10{10-12-17} cm from back of Heel, ending by working Rnd 2.

TOE
Rnd 1 (Decrease rnd)**:** K1, SSK, knit across first needle to last 3 sts, K2 tog, K1; with the second needle, K1, SSK, work across in pattern to last 3 sts, K2 tog, K1: 10{12-14-16} sts on **each** needle.

Rnd 2: Knit around.

Repeat Rnds 1 and 2, 2{2-3-4} times: 6{8-8-8} sts on **each** needle.

Cut yarn leaving a long end.

Graft remaining stitches together *(Figs. 17a & b, page 77)*.

Repeat for second Sock.

Design by Cathy Hardy.

child's vest

Child Size	Finished Chest Measurement	
4	26½"	(67.5 cm)
6	28½"	(72.5 cm)
8	30½"	(77.5 cm)
10	33"	(84 cm)
12	35"	(89 cm)
14	37"	(94 cm)

Size Note: Instructions are written with sizes 4, 6, and 8 in the first set of braces { } and sizes 10, 12, and 14 in the second set of braces. Instructions will be easier to read if you circle all the numbers pertaining to your size. If only one number is given, it applies to all sizes.

MATERIALS

Medium Weight Yarn
[3.5 ounces, 220 yards
(100 grams, 201 meters) per hank]:
  {2-2-3}{3-4-5} hanks
Straight knitting needles, sizes 6 (4 mm) **and** 7 (4.5 mm) **or** sizes needed for gauge
Stitch holder
Yarn needle

GAUGE: With larger size needles, in pattern, 7 repeats (21 sts) = 3¾" (9.5 cm)

Gauge Swatch: 4½" (11.5 cm) wide
With larger size needles, cast on 25 sts.
Work same as Back Body, Rows 1-4, page 10, for 4" (10 cm).
Bind off all sts in **knit**.

STITCH GUIDE
FRONT CROSS
Knit into the **front** of second st on left needle, then knit the first st letting both sts drop off the needle *(Figs. 3a & b, page 74)*.
BACK CROSS
Knit into the **back** loop of second st on left needle, then knit the first st letting both sts drop off the needle *(Figs. 4a & b, page 74)*.

When forming both Cross stitches, be sure to place the first new stitch all the way onto the shaft of the right needle.

BACK
RIBBING
With smaller size needles, cast on {76-82-88} {94-100-106} sts.

Work in K1, P1 ribbing for {2-2-2}{2½-2½-2½}" /{5-5-5}{6.5-6.5-6.5} cm.

Instructions continued on page 40.

BODY

Change to larger size needles.

Row 1: K1, (P2, K1) across.

Row 2 (Right side): P1, (work Front Cross, P1) across.

Row 3: K1, (P2, K1) across.

Row 4: P1, (work Back Cross, P1) across.

Repeat Rows 1-4 for pattern until Back measures approximately {8-8½-10} {11½-12-12½}"/{20.5-21.5-25.5}{29-30.5-32} cm from cast on edge, ending by working a **right** side row.

ARMHOLE SHAPING

Maintain established pattern throughout.

Rows 1 and 2: Bind off 6 sts, work across: {64-70-76}{82-88-94} sts.

Work even until Back measures approximately {14-15-17}{19-20-21}"/{35.5-38-43} {48.5-51-53.5} cm from cast on edge, ending by working a **right** side row.

Bind off all sts in pattern.

FRONT

Work same as Back until Front measures approximately {12-12½-14½}{16½-17¼-18}"/ {30.5-32-37}{42-44-45.5} cm from cast on edge, ending by working Row 1 of Body.

NECK SHAPING

Both sides of Neck are worked at the same time, using separate yarn for **each** side. The specified decreases will help maintain the cable pattern until both stitches forming the cable have been decreased.

Row 1: P1, (work Front Cross, P1) {7-8-8-} {9-9-10} times, slip next {20-20-26}{26-32-32} sts onto st holder; with second yarn, P1, (work Front Cross, P1) across: {22-25-25}{28-28-31} sts **each** side.

Row 2: K1, (P2, K1) across to within 3 sts of Neck edge, SSP *(Fig. 14, page 76)*, K1; with second yarn, K1, SSP, K1, (P2, K1) across: {21-24-24}{27-27-30} sts **each** side.

Row 3: P1, (work Back Cross, P1) across to within 2 sts of Neck edge, K1, P1; with second yarn, P1, K1, P1, (work Back Cross, P1) across.

Row 4: (K1, P2) across to within 3 sts of Neck edge, SSP, K1; with second yarn, K1, P2 tog *(Fig. 12, page 76)*, (P2, K1) across: {20-23-23}{26-26-29} sts **each** side.

Row 5: (P1, work Front Cross) across to within 2 sts of Neck edge, K1, P1; with second yarn, P1, K1, (work Front Cross, P1) across.

Row 6: K1, (P2, K1) across to within 4 sts of Neck edge, P1, P2 tog, K1; with second yarn, K1, P2 tog, P1, K1, (P2, K1) across: {19-22-22} {25-25-28} sts **each** side.

Row 7: P1, (work Back Cross, P1) across; with second yarn, P1, (work Back Cross, P1) across.

Row 8: K1, (P2, K1) across; with second yarn, K1, (P2, K1) across.

Row 9: P1, (work Front Cross, P1) across; with second yarn, P1, (work Front Cross, P1) across.

Row 10: K1, (P2, K1) across; with second yarn, K1, (P2, K1) across.

Repeat Rows 7-10 until Front measures same as Back, ending by working a **right** side row.

Bind off all sts in pattern.

NECK RIBBING

Sew left shoulder seam.

With **right** side facing and using smaller size needles, leave {19-22-22}{25-25-28} sts unworked for shoulder and pick up {26-26-32} {32-38-38} sts across Back neck edge *(Figs. 15a & b, page 76)*; pick up {12-14-14}{14-16-18} sts evenly spaced along left Front Neck edge, slip {20-20-26}{26-32-32} sts from Front st holder onto empty needle and knit across, pick up {12-14-14}{14-16-18} sts evenly spaced along right Front Neck edge: {70-74-86}{86-102-106} sts.

Work in K1, P1 ribbing for 1" (2.5 cm).

Bind off all sts **loosely** in ribbing.

Sew right shoulder and ribbing seam.

ARMHOLE RIBBING

With **right** side facing and using smaller size needles, pick up {58-64-70}{76-82-88} sts evenly spaced across end of rows along armhole edge, making sure **not** to pick up bound off sts.

Work in K1, P1 ribbing for 1" (2.5 cm).

Bind off all sts in ribbing.

Sew end of rows on ribbing to bound off stitches of Armhole.

Repeat for second Armhole.

Weave side seams *(Fig 16, page 77)*.

Design by Cathy Hardy.

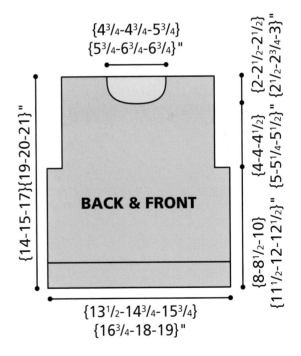

{4³/₄-4³/₄-5³/₄}
{5³/₄-6³/₄-6³/₄}"

{14-15-17}{19-20-21}"

{2-2¹/₂-2¹/₂}
{2¹/₂-2³/₄-3}"

{4-4-4¹/₂}
{5-5¹/₄-5¹/₂}"

{8-8¹/₂-10}
{11¹/₂-12-12¹/₂}"

BACK & FRONT

{13¹/₂-14³/₄-15³/₄}
{16³/₄-18-19}"

Note: Vest includes two edge stitches.

infant's pullover

Infant Size	Finished Chest Measurement	
3 months	18"	(45.5 cm)
6 months	19¹⁄₄"	(49 cm)
12 months	20³⁄₄"	(52.5 cm)
18 months	22"	(56 cm)
24 months	23¹⁄₂"	(59.5 cm)

Size Note: Instructions are written for size 3 months, with sizes 6, 12, 18, and 24 months in braces { }. Instructions will be easier to read if you circle all the numbers pertaining to your size. If only one number is given, it applies to all sizes.

MATERIALS

Medium Weight Yarn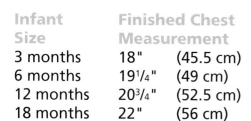
[3.52 ounces, 166 yards
(100 grams, 152 meters) per skein]:
    2{2-3-3-3} skeins
Straight knitting needles, sizes 6 (4 mm) **and**
    8 (5 mm) **or** sizes needed for gauge
Circular knitting needles, sizes 6 (4 mm) **and**
    7 (4.5 mm)
Split-ring markers (optional)
⁵⁄₈" (16 mm) Buttons - 2
Sewing needle and thread
Yarn needle

GAUGE: With larger size needles,
    in broken rib pattern,
    22 sts and 26 rows = 4" (10 cm)

Gauge Swatch: 4" (10 cm) square
Cast on 22 sts.
Row 1 (Right side)**:** Knit across.
Row 2: (K1, P1) across.
Rows 3-26: Repeat Rows 1 and 2 , 12 times.
Bind off all sts.

BACK
RIBBING

With smaller size straight needles, cast on 51{55-59-63-67} sts.

Row 1: K1, (P1, K1) across.

Row 2: P1, (K1, P1) across.

Repeat Rows 1 and 2, 2{2-3-4-4} times; then repeat Row 1 once **more**.

Instructions continued on page 44.

FITS INFANT
10 MONTHS

BODY

Change to larger size straight needles.

Row 1 (Right side)**:** Knit across.

Row 2: K1, (P1, K1) across.

Repeat Rows 1 and 2 for broken rib pattern until Back measures approximately 9{10-10½-11-12}"/23{25.5-26.5-28-30.5} cm from cast on edge, ending by working Row 2.

Bind off all sts in **knit**.

FRONT

Work same as Back until Front measures approximately 5½{6-6¼-6¼-6½}"/14{15-16-16-16.5} cm from cast on edge, ending by working Row 2.

PLACKET SHAPING

Both sides of Neck are worked at the same time, using separate yarn for **each** side.

Row 1: Knit 23{25-27-29-31} sts, bind off **next** 5 sts, knit across: 23{25-27-29-31} sts **each** side.

Row 2: K1, (P1, K1) across; with second yarn, K1, (P1, K1) across.

Row 3: Knit across; with second yarn, knit across.

Rows 4 thru 14{16-16-18-20}: Repeat Rows 2 and 3, 5{6-6-7-8} times; then repeat Row 2 once **more**.

NECK SHAPING
Maintain established pattern throughout.

Rows 1 and 2: Work across; with second yarn, bind off 4{5-5-5-5} sts, work across: 19{20-22-24-26} sts **each** side.

Row 3 (Decrease row)**:** Knit across to within 2 sts of Neck edge, K2 tog *(Fig. 9, page 75)*; with second yarn, SSK *(Figs. 10a-c, page 75)*, knit across: 18{19-21-23-25} sts **each** side.

Row 4: Work across; with second yarn, work across.

Repeat Rows 3 and 4, 1{1-1-1-2} time(s): 17{18-20-22-23} sts **each** side.

Work even until Front measures same as Back, ending by working a **wrong** side row.

Bind off all sts in **knit**.

Sew shoulder seams.

Using split-ring markers or scrap yarn, place a marker on **each** side of Front and Back 4{4½-5-5¼-5½}"/10{11.5-12.5-13.5-14} cm down from shoulder seam.

SLEEVE
BODY

With **right** side facing and using larger size straight needles, pick up 44{50-56-58-60} sts evenly spaced between markers **(Fig. 15a, page 76)**; remove markers.

Row 1: (K1, P1) across.

Row 2: Knit across.

Rows 3-7: Repeat Rows 1 and 2 twice, then repeat Row 1 once **more**.

Row 8 (Decrease row)**:** SSK, knit across to last 2 sts, K2 tog: 42{48-54-56-58} sts.

Continue to decrease one stitch at each edge, every fourth row, 5{3-4-5-8} times; then decrease every other row, 2{7-8-7-5} times: 28{28-30-32-32} sts.

Work even until Sleeve measures approximately 6{6^1/$_2$-7^1/$_2$-8^1/$_2$-9^1/$_2$}"/ 15{16.5-19-21.5-24} cm.

RIBBING

Change to smaller size straight needles.

Work in K1, P1 ribbing for 7{7-9-11-11} rows.

Bind off all sts **loosely** in ribbing, leaving a long end for sewing.

Repeat for second Sleeve.

FINISHING
BUTTON BAND

With **right** side facing and using smaller size straight needles, pick up 15{17-17-19-21} sts evenly spaced across left Front Placket opening for Girl's **or** right Front Placket opening for Boy's.

Row 1: K1, (P1, K1) across.

Row 2: P1, (K1, P1) across.

Rows 3-5: Repeat Rows 1 and 2 once, then repeat Row 1 once **more**.

Bind off all sts in established ribbing.

BUTTONHOLE BAND

With **right** side facing and using smaller size straight needles, pick up 15{17-17-19-21} sts evenly spaced across remaining Front Placket opening.

Row 1: K1, (P1, K1) across.

Row 2: P1, (K1, P1) across.

Girl's Only - Row 3 (Buttonhole row)**:** K1, P2 tog **(Fig. 12, page 76)**, YO **(Fig. 6b, page 74)**, (P1, K1) 2{3-3-3-4} times, P2 tog, YO, (P1, K1) across.

Boy's Only - Row 3 (Buttonhole row)**:** K1, (P1, K1) 2{2-2-3-3} times, P2 tog **(Fig. 12, page 76)**, YO **(Fig. 6b, page 74)**, (P1, K1) 2{3-3-3-4} times, P2 tog, YO, P1, K1.

Rows 4 and 5: Work in established ribbing across.

Bind off all sts in established ribbing.

Sew bottom edge of Bands to bound off edge on Front Placket Opening, placing Buttonhole Band over Button Band.

Instructions continued on page 49.

T-sweater

▬▬☐☐ **EASY**

Child Size	Finished Chest Measurement	
2	26"	(66 cm)
4	27"	(68.5 cm)
6	28"	(71 cm)
8	29½"	(75 cm)
10	31"	(78.5 cm)

Size Note: Instructions are written for size 2 with sizes 4, 6, 8, and 10 in braces { }. Instructions will be easier to read if you circle all the numbers pertaining to your size. If only one number is given, it applies to all sizes.

MATERIALS
Medium Weight Yarn **(🌀4)** MEDIUM
[3.5 ounces, 170 yards
(100 grams, 156 meters) per skein]:
  4{4-4-5-6} skeins
Circular knitting needles, sizes 7 (4.5 mm)
  and 9 (5.5 mm) **or** sizes needed for gauge
Yarn needle

GAUGE: With larger size needle, in pattern,
  18 sts = 3¾" (9.5 cm)

Gauge Swatch: 4" (10 cm) square
With larger size needle, cast on 19 sts.
Work same as Back Body, Rows 1 and 2
for 4" (10 cm).
Bind off all sts in **knit**.

BACK
BODY
With smaller size needle, cast on
64{67-70-73-76} sts.

Row 1 (Right side): P1, (K2, P1) across.

Row 2: K1, (YO, K2, pass YO over last 2 sts, K1) across **(Fig. 6a, page 74)**.

Repeat Rows 1 and 2 for pattern until piece measures approximately 2" (5 cm) from cast on edge, ending by working Row 2.

Instructions continued on page 48.

T-sweater

Change to larger size needles.

Continue to repeat Rows 1 and 2 until piece measures approximately 8¹/₂{9¹/₂-10¹/₂-11¹/₂-12¹/₂}"/21.5{24-26.5-29-32} cm from cast on edge, ending by working Row 2.

SLEEVES
Row 1: Add on 33{36-39-42-45} sts *(Figs. 7a & b, page 75)*, P1, (K2, P1) across: 97{103-109-115-121} sts.

Row 2: Add on 33{36-39-42-45} sts, K1, (YO, K2, pass YO over last 2 sts, K1) across: 130{139-148-157-166} sts.

Repeat Rows 1 and 2 of Body until Sleeves measure approximately 5¹/₂{6-6¹/₂-7-7¹/₂}"/14{15-16.5-18-19} cm, ending by working Row 2.

Bind off all sts loosely in pattern.

FRONT
Work same as Back.

FINISHING
Weave side and underarm in one continuous seam *(Fig. 16, page 77)*.

Sew seam across top edge, leaving a 7{7-7¹/₂-7¹/₂-8¹/₂}"/18{18-19-19-21.5} cm neck opening.

Design by Cathy Hardy.

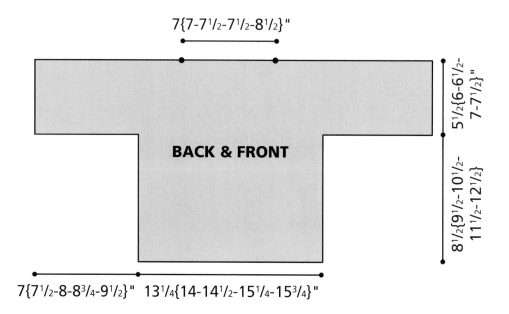

7{7-7¹/₂-7¹/₂-8¹/₂}"

BACK & FRONT

5¹/₂{6-6¹/₂-7-7¹/₂}"

8¹/₂{9¹/₂-10¹/₂-11¹/₂-12¹/₂}

7{7¹/₂-8-8³/₄-9¹/₂}" 13¹/₄{14-14¹/₂-15¹/₄-15³/₄}"

Note: Sweater includes two edge stitches.

COLLAR

With **right** side facing and using smaller size circular needle, pick up 20{20-22-24-26} sts evenly spaced along right Front Neck edge **(Fig. 15b, page 76)**, pick up 17{19-19-19-21} sts across Back Neck edge, pick up 20{20-22-24-26} sts evenly spaced along left Front Neck edge: 57{59-63-67-73} sts.

Row 1: K1, (P1, K1) across.

Row 2: P1, (K1, P1) across.

Repeat Rows 1 and 2 for ³/₄{³/₄-1-1-1}"/ 2{2-2.5-2.5-2.5} cm.

Change to larger size circular needle.

Repeat Rows 1 and 2 until Collar measures 1¹/₂{1¹/₂-2-2-2}"/4{4-5-5-5} cm.

Bind off all sts **loosely** in established ribbing.

Weave underarm and side in one continuous seam **(Fig. 16, page 77)**.

Sew buttons to Button Band opposite buttonholes.

Design by Cathy Hardy.

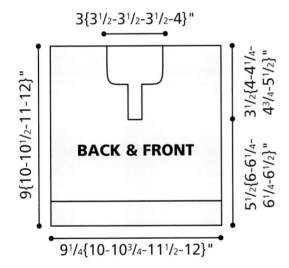

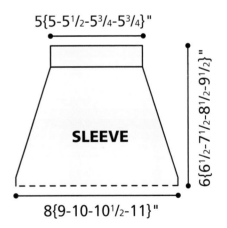

Note: Pullover includes two edge stitches.

child's sweater

Child Size	Finished Chest Measurement	
2	23"	(58.5 cm)
4	25"	(63.5 cm)
6	26½"	(67.5 cm)
8	28½"	(72.5 cm)
10	30"	(76 cm)
12	32"	(81.5 cm)

Size Note: Instructions are written with sizes 2, 4, and 6 in the first set of braces { } and sizes 8, 10, and 12 in the second set of braces. Instructions will be easier to read if you circle all the numbers pertaining to your size. If only one number is given, it applies to all sizes.

MATERIALS
Medium Weight Yarn
[3.52 ounces, 166 yards
(100 grams, 152 meters) per skein]:
    Main Color (Pink) - {2-3-3}{3-4-4} skeins
    Contrasting Color (Purple) - 1 skein
Straight knitting needles, sizes 6 (4 mm) **and** 8 (5 mm) **or** sizes needed for gauge
Stitch holder
Split-ring markers (optional)
Yarn needle

GAUGE: With larger size needles,
            in Stockinette Stitch,
            18 sts and 24 rows = 4" (10 cm)

BACK
RIBBING
With smaller size needles and Main Color, cast on {54-58-62}{66-70-74} sts.

Work in K1, P1 ribbing for {2-2-2}{2½-2½-2½}"/{5-5-5}{6.5-6.5-6.5} cm.

BODY
Change to larger size needles.

Beginning with a **purl** row, work in Stockinette Stitch (purl one row, knit one row) until Back measures approximately {14¼-15¾-17¼}{18¼-19-20¼}"/{36-40-44}{46.5-48.5-51.5} cm from cast on edge, ending by working a **purl** row.

Bind off all sts in **knit**.

FRONT
RIBBING
Work same as Back.

BODY
Change to larger size needles.

Row 1: Purl across.

Row 2 (Right side)**:** Knit across.

Instructions continued on page 52.

Row 3: P2, ★ YO *(Fig. 6b, page 74)*, P2, pass YO over last 2 sts, P2; repeat from ★ across.

Carry unused color along side of piece.

Row 4: With Contrasting Color knit across.

Row 5: P4, YO, P2, pass YO over last 2 sts, ★ P2, YO, P2, pass YO over last 2 sts; repeat from ★ across to last 4 sts, P4.

Row 6: With Main Color knit across.

Repeat Rows 3-6 for pattern until Front measures approximately {11³/₄-13¹/₄-14³/₄} {15³/₄-16¹/₂-17³/₄}"/{30-33.5-37.5}{40-42-45} cm from cast on edge, ending by working Row 6.

NECK SHAPING

Both sides of Neck are worked at the same time, using separate yarn for **each** side. Maintain established pattern and color sequence throughout.

Row 1: Work across {22-24-26}{28-29-31} sts, slip next {10-10-10}{10-12-12} sts onto st holder; with second yarn, work across: {22-24-26}{28-29-31} sts **each** side.

Row 2 (Decrease row)**:** Knit across to within 2 sts of Neck edge, K2 tog *(Fig. 9, page 75)*; with second yarn, SSK *(Figs. 10a-c, page 75)*, knit across: {21-23-25}{27-28-30} sts **each** side.

Row 3: Work across; with second yarn, work across.

Repeat Rows 2 and 3, {2-2-3}{3-3-3} times, then repeat Row 2 once **more**: {18-20-21}{23-24-26} sts **each** side.

Work even until Front measures same as Back, ending by working a **knit** row.

Bind off all sts in **purl**.

NECK RIBBING

Sew left shoulder seam.

With **right** side facing, using smaller size needles and Main Color, leave {18-20-21} {23-24-26} sts unworked for shoulder and pick up {18-18-20}{20-22-22} sts across Back neck edge *(Figs. 15a & b, page 76)*, pick up 15 sts evenly spaced along left Front Neck edge, knit {10-10-10}{10-12-12} sts from Front st holder, pick up 15 sts evenly spaced along right Front Neck edge: {58-58-60}{60-64-64} sts.

Work in K1, P1 ribbing for 1" (2.5 cm).

Bind off all sts **loosely** in ribbing.

Sew right shoulder and ribbing seam.

Using split-ring markers or scrap yarn, place a marker on **each** side of Front and Back {5¹/₄-5³/₄-6¹/₄}{6³/₄-7-7¹/₄}"/{13.5-14.5-16} {17-18-18.5} cm down from shoulder seam.

SLEEVE
BODY

With **right** side facing, using larger size needles and Main Color, pick up {48-52-56}{60-64-66} sts evenly spaced between markers.

Beginning with a **purl** row, work in Stockinette Stitch for 1" (2.5 cm), ending by working a **purl** row.

SHAPING

Row 1 (Decrease row): SSK, knit across to last 2 sts, K2 tog: {46-50-54}{58-62-64} sts.

Continue to decrease one stitch at each edge, every tenth row, {1-2-1}{4-4-8} time(s); then decrease every eight row, {5-5-7}{4-5-1} time(s): {34-36-38}{42-44-46} sts.

Work even in Stockinette Stitch until Sleeve measures approximately {10-11¼-12½} {13½-15-16½}"/{25.5-28.5-32}{34.5-38-42} cm.

RIBBING

Change to smaller size needles.

Work in K1, P1 ribbing across decreasing {4-4-4}{6-6-6} sts evenly spaced: {30-32-34} {36-38-40} sts.

Work in established ribbing for {1½-1½-1½} {2-2-2}"/{4-4-4}{5-5-5} cm.

Bind off all sts **loosely** in ribbing.

Repeat for second Sleeve.

FINISHING

Weave underarm and side in one continuous seam **(Fig. 16, page 77)**.

Design by Kay Meadors.

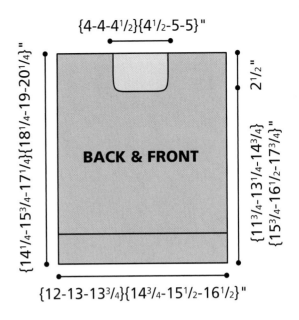

{4-4-4½}{4½-5-5}"

2½"

{11¾-13¼-14¾} {15¾-16½-17¾}"

{14¼-15¾-17¼}{18¼-19-20¼}"

BACK & FRONT

{12-13-13¾}{14¾-15½-16½}"

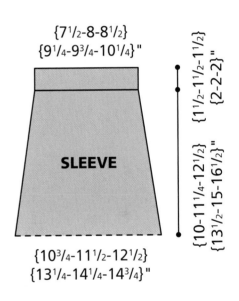

{7½-8-8½} {9¼-9¾-10¼}"

{1½-1½-1½} {2-2-2}"

SLEEVE

{10-11¼-12½} {13½-15-16½}"

{10¾-11½-12½} {13¼-14¼-14¾}"

Note: Sweater includes two edge stitches.

mariner's vest

 EASY

Adult Size	Finished Chest Measurement	
34	37½"	(95.5 cm)
36	39½"	(100.5 cm)
38	41½"	(105.5 cm)
40	43"	(109 cm)
42	45"	(114.5 cm)
44	47"	(119.5 cm)

Size Note: Instructions are written with sizes 34, 36, and 38 in the first set of braces { } and sizes 40, 42, and 44 in the second set of braces. Instructions will be easier to read if you circle all the numbers pertaining to your size. If only one number is given, it applies to all sizes.

MATERIALS
Medium Weight Yarn **(4)**
[5 ounces, 260 yards
(141 grams, 238 meters) per skein]:
  {3-3-3}{3-3-4} skeins
Straight knitting needles, sizes 7 (4.5 mm)
  and 10 (6 mm) **or** sizes needed for gauge
Stitch holder
Yarn needle

When instructed to slip a stitch, always slip as if to **purl** with yarn held loosely to **wrong** side.

GAUGE: With larger size needles, in pattern, 17 sts = 4" (10 cm)

Gauge Swatch: 4¼" (10.75 cm) square
With larger size needles, cast on 18 sts.
Row 1: Purl across.
Row 2 (Right side)**:** K2, (slip 1, K1) across.
Row 3: P2, (slip 1, P1) across.
Repeat Rows 2 and 3 for pattern for 4¼" (10.75 cm).
Bind off all sts.

BACK
RIBBING
With smaller size needles, cast on {82-86-90}{94-98-102} sts.

Work in K1, P1 ribbing for 2" (5 cm).

BODY
Change to larger size needles.

Row 1 (Right side)**:** K2, (slip 1, K1) across.

Row 2: P2, (slip 1, P1) across.

Repeat Rows 1 and 2 for pattern until Back measures approximately 15" (38 cm) from cast on edge, ending by working Row 2.

ARMHOLE SHAPING
Row 1: Bind off 6 sts, K1, (slip 1, K1) across: {76-80-84}{88-92-96} sts.

Row 2: Bind off 6 sts, P1, (slip 1, P1) across: {70-74-78}{82-86-90} sts.

Row 3 (Decrease row)**:** K1, SSK *(Figs. 10a-c, page 75)*, (K1, slip 1) across to last 3 sts, K2 tog *(Fig. 9, page 75)*, K1: {68-72-76}{80-84-88} sts.

Row 4: (P1, slip 1) across to last 2 sts, P2.

Row 5 (Decrease row)**:** K1, SSK, (slip 1, K1) across to last 3 sts, K2 tog, K1: {66-70-74}{78-82-86} sts.

Row 6: P2, (slip 1, P1) across.

Rows 7-10: Repeat Rows 3-6: {62-66-70}{74-78-82} sts.

Row 11: K2, (slip 1, K1) across.

Row 12: P2, (slip 1, P1) across.

Rows 13 and 14: Repeat Rows 3 and 4: {60-64-68}{72-76-80} sts.

Row 15: (K1, slip 1) across to last 2 sts, K2.

Rows 16-18: Repeat Rows 4-6: {58-62-66}{70-74-78} sts.

Rows 19-26: Repeat Rows 11-18: {54-58-62}{66-70-74} sts.

Rows 27-29: Repeat Rows 11-13: {52-56-60}{64-68-72} sts.

Instructions continued on page 56.

Row 30: (P1, slip 1) across to last 2 sts, P2.

Row 31: (K1, slip 1) across to last 2 sts, K2.

Repeat Rows 30 and 31 until Back measures approximately {24½-24¾-25}{25¼-25½-25¾}"/ {62-63-63.5}{64-65-65.5} cm from cast on edge, ending by working a **wrong** side row.

Bind off all sts in **knit**.

FRONT

Work same as Back until Front measures approximately {20½-20¾-21}{21¼-21½-21¾}"/ {52-52.5-53.5}{54-54.5-55} cm from cast on edge, ending by working a **wrong** side row: {52-56-60}{64-68-72} sts.

NECK SHAPING

Both sides of Neck are worked at the same time, using separate yarn for **each** side.

Row 1: K1, (slip 1, K1) {9-10-10}{11-12-13} times, slip next {14-14-18}{18-18-18} sts onto st holder; with second yarn, K2, slip 1, (K1, slip 1) across to last 2 sts, K2: {19-21-21}{23-25-27} sts **each** side.

Row 2: P1, (slip 1, P1) across; with second yarn, P2, slip 1, (P1, slip 1) across to last 2 sts, P2.

Row 3 (Decrease row): (K1, slip 1) across to within 3 sts of Neck edge, K2 tog, K1; with second yarn, K1, SSK, (K1, slip 1) across to last 2 sts, K2: {18-20-20}{22-24-26} sts **each** side.

Row 4: (P1, slip 1) across to within 2 sts of Neck edge, P2; with second yarn, (P1, slip 1) across to last 2 sts, P2.

Row 5 (Decrease row): K1, (slip 1, K1) across to within 3 sts of Neck edge, K2 tog, K1; with second yarn, K1, SSK, slip 1, (K1, slip 1) across to last 2 sts, K2: {17-19-19}{21-23-25} sts **each** side.

Rows 6-8: Repeat Rows 2-4: {16-18-18} {20-22-24} sts **each** side.

Row 9: (K1, slip 1) across to within 2 sts of Neck edge, K2; with second yarn, (K1, slip 1) across to last 2 sts, K2.

Rows 10 and 11: Repeat Rows 4 and 5: {15-17-17}{19-21-23} sts **each** side.

Row 12: P1, (slip 1, P1) across; with second yarn, P2, slip 1, (P1, slip 1) across to last 2 sts, P2.

Row 13: K1, (slip 1, K1) across; with second yarn, K2, slip 1, (K1, slip 1) across to last 2 sts, K2.

Rows 14-16: Repeat Rows 2-4: {14-16-16}{18-20-22} sts **each** side

Row 17: (K1, slip 1) across to within 2 sts of Neck edge, K2; with second yarn, (K1, slip 1) across to last 2 sts, K2.

Rows 18 and 19: Repeat Rows 4 and 5: {13-15-15}{17-19-21} sts **each** side.

Repeat Rows 12 and 13 until Front measures same as Back, ending by working a **wrong** side row.

Bind off all sts in **knit**.

NECK RIBBING

Sew left shoulder seam.

With **right** side facing and using smaller size needles, leave {13-15-15}{17-19-21} sts unworked for shoulder and pick up {26-26-30}{30-30-30} sts across Back neck edge *(Figs. 15a & b, page 76)*; pick up 18 sts evenly spaced along left Front Neck edge, slip {14-14-18}{18-18-18} sts from Front st holder onto empty needle and knit across, pick up 18 sts evenly spaced along right Front Neck edge: {76-76-84}{84-84-84} sts.

Work in K1, P1 ribbing for 1" (2.5 cm).

Bind off all sts **loosely** in ribbing.

Sew right shoulder and ribbing seam.

ARMHOLE RIBBING

With **right** side facing and using smaller size needles, pick up {94-96-100}{102-104-106} sts evenly spaced across armhole edge.

Work in K1, P1 ribbing for 1" (2.5 cm).

Bind off all sts in ribbing.

Repeat for second Armhole.

Weave side seams *(Fig. 16, page 77)*.

Design by Cathy Hardy.

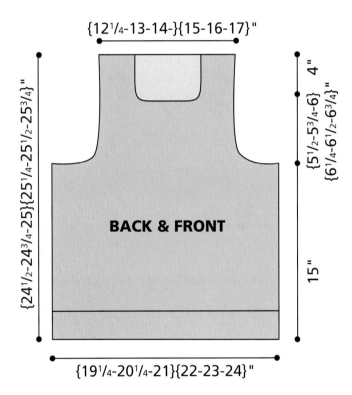

Note: Vest includes two edge stitches.

baby blanket

Finished Size: 40" (101.5 cm) square

MATERIALS

Medium Weight Yarn (🔵4)
[6 ounces, 315 yards
(170 grams, 288 meters) per skein]:
  5 skeins
29" (73.5 cm) Circular knitting needle,
  size 8 (5 mm) **or** size needed for gauge

GAUGE: In Garter Stitch, 18 sts = 3½" (9 cm)
        in pattern,
        6 repeats (24 sts) = 3½" (9 cm)

Measure gauge while your swatch is relaxed.

Gauge Swatch: 3¾" (9.5 cm) square
Cast on 26 sts.
Row 1 (Right side)**:** P2, (K2, P2) across.
Row 2: K2, (P2, K2) across.
Row 3: P2, (work Front Cross, P2) across.
Row 4: K2, (P2, K2) across.
Repeat Rows 1-4 for pattern for 3¾" (9.5 cm).
Bind off all sts in pattern.

STITCH GUIDE

FRONT CROSS

Knit into the **front** of second st on left
needle, then knit the first st letting both sts
drop off the needle (*Figs. 3a & b, page 74*).

When forming Cross stitches, be sure to
place the first new stitch all the way onto
the shaft of the right needle.

BODY

Cast on 205 sts.

Rows 1-6: Knit across.

Increases are made by knitting into the front
and into the back of the next st (*Figs. 8a & b,
page 75*).

Row 7 (Increase row)**:** K6, increase, (K2,
increase) across to last 6 sts, K6: 270 sts.

Row 8 (Right side)**:** K4, P2, (K2, P2) across to
last 4 sts, K4.

Row 9: K6, P2, (K2, P2) across to last 6 sts, K6.

Row 10: K4, P2, (work Front Cross, P2) across
to last 4 sts, K4.

Row 11: K6, P2, (K2, P2) across to last 6 sts,
K6.

Repeat Rows 8-11 for pattern until blanket
measures approximately 39" (99 cm) from cast
on edge, ending by working Row 8.

Next Row (Decrease row)**:** K6, P2 tog (*Fig. 12,
page 76*), (K2, P2 tog) across to last 6 sts, K6:
205 sts.

Last 6 Rows: Knit across.

Bind off all sts in **knit**.

Design by Cathy Hardy.

⬛⬛◻◻◻ EASY

Finished Size: 48" x 60" (122 cm x 152.5 cm)

MATERIALS

Medium Weight Yarn **(4)** MEDIUM
[3 ounces, 158 yards
(85 grams, 144 meters) per skein]:
   12 skeins
Circular knitting needle, size 9 (5.5 mm) **or**
   size needed for gauge

GAUGE: In Diagonal pattern,
   20 sts = 3³/₄" (9.5 cm)

Gauge Swatch: 4" (10 cm) square
Cast on 21 sts.
Rows 1-17: Work same as Body Rows 9 and
10, 8 times; then repeat Row 9 once **more**.
Bind off all sts in **knit**.

STITCH GUIDE

BACK CROSS
Knit into the **back** loop of second st on
left needle, then knit the first st letting
both sts drop off the needle *(Figs. 4a & b,
page 74)*.

FRONT CROSS
Knit into the **front** of second st on left
needle, then knit the first st letting both
sts drop off the needle *(Figs. 3a & b,
page 74)*.

PURL CROSS
Purl into the **front** of second st on left
needle, then purl the first st letting both
sts drop off the needle *(Figs. 5a & b,
page 74)*.

When forming all Cross stitches, be sure to
place the first new stitch all the way onto
the shaft of the right needle.

BODY
Cast on 255 sts.

Row 1: K2, work Back Cross across to last st,
K1.

Row 2: K2, work Front Cross across to last st,
K1.

Rows 3-8: Repeat Rows 1 and 2, 3 times for
Garter pattern.

Row 9: P2, work Purl Cross across to last st, P1.

Row 10 (Right side)**:** K2, work Front Cross
across to last st, K1.

Repeat Rows 9 and 10 for Diagonal pattern for
12¹/₂" (32 cm).

Beginning again with Row 1, alternate
working both patterns until a total of
5 Garter patterns have been worked, ending
by working a Garter pattern.

Bind off all sts in **knit**.

Design by Cathy Hardy.

animal's blanket

Finished Size: 36" (91.5 cm) square

MATERIALS

Medium Weight Yarn 🧶**4**
[7 ounces, 364 yards
(198 grams, 333 meters) per skein]:
  4 skeins
  Note: Scrap yarn from other projects
    can be used.
Circular knitting needles, sizes 11 (8 mm) **and**
  13 (9 mm) **or** sizes needed for gauge

Entire blanket is worked holding two strands
of yarn together.

GAUGE: With larger size needle, in pattern,
      14 sts = 4" (10 cm);
      10 rows = $3^3/_4$" (9.5 cm)

Gauge Swatch: $4^1/_4$"w x $3^3/_4$"h
(10.75 cm x 9.5 cm)
With larger size needle and holding two
strands of yarn together, cast on 15 sts.
Rows 1-10: Work same as Body Rows 4 and 5,
5 times.
Bind off all sts in **knit**.

STITCH GUIDE

BACK CROSS

Knit into the **back** loop of second st on left
needle, then knit the first st letting both sts
drop off the needle **(Figs. 4a & b, page 74)**.

PURL CROSS

Purl into the **front** of second st on left
needle, then purl the first st letting both sts
drop off the needle **(Figs. 5a & b, page 74)**.

When forming both Cross stitches, be sure
to place the first new stitch all the way
onto the shaft of the right needle.

BODY

With smaller size needle and holding two
strands of yarn together, cast on 127 sts.

Rows 1-3: Knit across.

Change to larger size needle.

Row 4 (Right side)**:** K3, work Back Cross across
to last 2 sts, K2.

Row 5: K2, P1, work Purl Cross across to last
2 sts, K2.

Repeat Rows 4 and 5 for pattern until blanket
measures approximately $35^1/_4$" (89.5 cm) from
cast on edge, ending by working Row 4.

Last 3 Rows: With smaller size needle, knit
across.

Bind off all sts in **knit** leaving a long end for
weaving in end.

Double knot all of the ends and weave them
into the blanket so that it can withstand
washing and wear.

Design by Cathy Hardy.

bulky sweater

Size	Finished Chest Measurement	
Children		
10	32"	(81.5 cm)
12	34"	(86.5 cm)
14	36"	(91.5 cm)
Adult		
34	38"	(96.5 cm)
36	40"	(101.5 cm)
38	42"	(106.5 cm)
40	44"	(112 cm)
42	46"	(117 cm)
44	48"	(122 cm)

Size Note: Instructions are written with sizes for Children in the first set of braces { }, with Adult sizes 34, 36, and 38 in the second set of braces, and sizes 40, 42, and 44 in the third set of braces. Instructions will be easier to read if you circle all the numbers pertaining to your size. If only one number is given, it applies to all sizes.

MATERIALS
Medium Weight Yarn 4
[3.5 ounces, 223 yards
(100 grams, 205 meters) per skein]:
 {4-5-6}{6-7-7}{8-8-9} skeins
Straight knitting needles, sizes 7 (4.5 mm)
 and 9 (5.5 mm) **or** sizes needed for gauge
Stitch holders - 2
Yarn needle

GAUGE: With larger size needles,
 in K1, P1 ribbing, 18 sts = 3" (7.5 cm)
 in pattern, 1 repeat (10 rows) = 2"
 (5 cm)

Measure gauge while piece is relaxed.

BACK
With smaller size needles, cast on {98-104-110} {116-122-128}{134-140-146} sts.

Row 1: (P1, K1) across to last 2 sts, P2.

Row 2 (Right side)**:** K2, (P1, K1) across.

Rows 3-6: Repeat Rows 1 and 2 twice.

Change to larger size needles.

Row 7 (Decrease row)**:** P1, SSP across to last st *(Fig. 14, page 76)*, P1: {50-53-56}{59-62-65} {68-71-74} sts.

Row 8: Knit across.

Row 9: Purl across.

Increases are made by knitting into the front and into the back of the next st *(Figs. 8a & b, page 75)*.

Row 10 (Increase row)**:** K1, increase in each st across to last st, K1: {98-104-110}{116-122-128} {134-140-146} sts.

Row 11: (P1, K1) across to last 2 sts, P2.

Row 12: K2, (P1, K1) across.

Rows 13-16: Repeat Rows 11 and 12 twice.

Repeat Rows 7-16 for pattern until piece measures approximately {20-22-24} {24-26-26}{26-28-28}"/ {51-56-61}{61-66-66} {66-71-71} cm from cast on edge, ending by working Row 8.

Last Row: Bind off {18-19-20}{21-22-23} {25-26-27} sts, purl across until there are {14-15-16} {17-18-19}{18-19-20} sts on the right needle then slip them onto st holder, bind off remaining sts.

FRONT
Work same as Back until Front measures approximately {16½-18½-20½} {20½-22½-22½} {22½-24½-24½}"/{42-47-52} {52-57-57}{57-62-62} cm from cast on edge, ending by working Row 10: {98-104-110}{116-122-128} {134-140-146} sts.

Instructions continued on page 66.

NECK SHAPING

Both sides of Neck are worked at the same time, using separate yarn for **each** side.

Row 1: (P1, K1) {19-20-21}{22-23-24}{26-27-28} times, SSP; slip next {18-20-22}{{24-26-28} {26-28-30} sts onto st holder; with second yarn, P2 tog *(Fig. 12, page 76)*, (P1, K1) across to last 2 sts, P2: {39-41-43}{45-47-49}{53-55-57} sts **each** side.

Row 2 (Decrease row)**:** K2, P1, (K1, P1) across to within 2 sts of Neck edge, K2 tog *(Fig. 9, page 75)*; with second yarn, SSK *(Figs. 10a-c, page 75)*, K1, (P1, K1) across: {38-40-42} {44-46-48}{52-54-56} sts **each** side.

Row 3 (Decrease row)**:** (P1, K1) across to within 4 sts of Neck edge, P2, SSP; with second yarn, P2 tog, (P1, K1) across to last 2 sts, P2: {37-39-41}{43-45-47}{51-53-55} sts **each** side.

Rows 4-6: Repeat Rows 2 and 3 once, then repeat Row 2 once **more**: {34-36-38}{40-42-44} {48-50-52} sts **each** side.

Row 7: P1, SSP across to within one st of Neck edge, P1; with second yarn, P1, SSP across to last st, P1: {18-19-20}{21-22-23}{25-26-27} sts **each** side.

Row 8: Knit across; with second yarn, knit across.

Row 9: Purl across; with second yarn, purl across.

Row 10: K1, increase in each st across to within one st of Neck edge, K1; with second yarn, K1, increase in each st across to last st, K1: {34-36-38}{40-42-44}{48-50-52} sts **each** side.

Row 11: (P1, K1) across to within 2 sts of neck edge, P2; with second yarn, (P1, K1) across to last 2 sts, P2.

Row 12: K2, (P1, K1) across; with second yarn, K2, (P1, K1) across.

Rows 13-16: Repeat Rows 11 and 12 twice.

Rows 17 and 18: Repeat Rows 7 and 8: {18-19-20}{21-22-23}{25-26-27} sts **each** side.

Bind off all sts in **purl.**

SLEEVE (Make 2)

With smaller size needles, cast on {46-52-52}{54-54-56}{62-62-64} sts.

Rows 1-11: Work same as Back.

Row 12: Increase, (K1, P1) across to last st, increase: {48-54-54}{56-56-58}{64-64-66} sts.

Row 13: P2, (K1, P1) across.

Row 14: Increase, (P1, K1) across to last st, increase: {50-56-56}{58-58-60}{66-66-68} sts.

Row 15: (P1, K1) across to last 2 sts, P2.

Row 16: Increase, (K1, P1) across to last st, increase: {52-58-58}{60-60-62}{68-68-70} sts.

Row 17 (Pattern decrease row)**:** P2, SSP across to last 2 sts, P2: {28-31-31}{32-32-33}{36-36-37} sts.

Row 18: Increase, knit across to last st, increase: {30-33-33}{34-34-35}{38-38-39} sts.

Row 19: Purl across.

Row 20 (Pattern increase row)**:** Increase, K2, increase in each st across to last 3 sts, K2, increase: {56-62-62}{64-64-66}{72-72-74} sts.

Row 21: P2, (K1, P1) across.

Row 22: Increase, (P1, K1) across to last st, increase: {58-64-64}{66-66-68}{74-74-76} sts.

Row 23: (P1, K1) across to last 2 sts, P2.

Row 24: Increase, (K1, P1) across to last st, increase: {60-66-66}{68-68-70}{76-76-78} sts.

Row 25: P2, (K1, P1) across.

Row 26: Increase, (P1, K1) across to last st, increase: {62-68-68}{70-70-72}{78-78-80} sts.

Row 27 (Pattern decrease row)**:** P3, SSP across to last st, P1: {33-36-36}{37-37-38}{41-41-42} sts.

Row 28: Increase, knit across to last st, increase: {35-38-38}{39-39-40}{43-43-44} sts.

Row 29: Purl across.

Row 30 (Pattern increase row)**:** Increase, K1, increase in each st across to last 4 sts, K3, increase: {66-72-72}{74-74-76}{82-82-84} sts.

Row 31: (P1, K1) across to last 2 sts, P2.

Continue to increase one stitch at each edge, in same manner (Rows 12-31), every other row, {9-6-8}{11-16-20}{19-24-27} times; then every fourth row, {3-6-7}{6-4-2}{3-1-0} time(s) **(see Zeros, page 72)**, working new sts in pattern: {90-96-102}{108-114-120}{126-132-138} sts on ribbing row.

Work even until Sleeve measures approximately {14-15¹/₂-17}{17¹/₂-18-18}{18¹/₄-18¹/₄-18¹/₂}"/{35.5-39.5-43}{44.5-45.5-45.5}{46.5-46.5-47} cm.

Bind off all sts in pattern.

Instructions continued on page 68.

FINISHING

Sew left shoulder seam.

NECK RIBBING

With **right** side facing, slip {14-15-16}{17-18-19} {18-19-20} sts from Back st holder onto smaller size needle and increase in each st across; pick up 22 sts evenly spaced along left Front Neck edge *(Fig. 15a, page 76)*, knit {18-20-22} {24-26-28}{26-28-30} sts from Front st holder, pick up 22 sts evenly spaced along right Front Neck edge: {90-94-98}{102-106-110} {106-110-114} sts.

Work in K1, P1 ribbing for 2" (5 cm).

Bind off all sts **loosely** in ribbing.

Sew right shoulder and ribbing seam. Fold Neck Ribbing to **wrong** side and sew bound off edge loosely in place.

Sew Sleeves to sweater, placing center of Sleeve at shoulder seam and beginning {7¹⁄₂-8-8¹⁄₂}{9-9¹⁄₂-10}{10¹⁄₂-11-11¹⁄₂}"/ {19-20.5-21.5}{23-24-25.5}{26.5-28-29} cm down from seam.

Weave underarm and side in one continuous seam *(Fig. 16, page 77)*.

Design by Cathy Hardy.

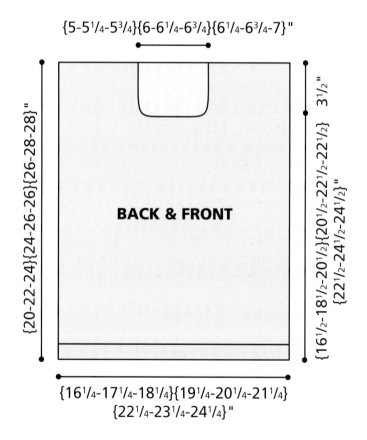

{5-5¹⁄₄-5³⁄₄}{6-6¹⁄₄-6³⁄₄}{6¹⁄₄-6³⁄₄-7}"

BACK & FRONT

{20-22-24}{24-26-26}{26-28-28}"

{16¹⁄₂-18¹⁄₂-20¹⁄₂}{20¹⁄₂-22¹⁄₂-22¹⁄₂} {22¹⁄₂-24¹⁄₂-24¹⁄₂}"

3¹⁄₂"

{16¹⁄₄-17¹⁄₄-18¹⁄₄}{19¹⁄₄-20¹⁄₄-21¹⁄₄} {22¹⁄₄-23¹⁄₄-24¹⁄₄}"

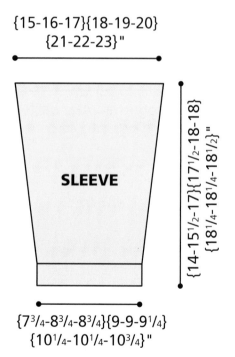

{15-16-17}{18-19-20} {21-22-23}"

SLEEVE

{14-15¹⁄₂-17}{17¹⁄₂-18-18} {18¹⁄₄-18¹⁄₄-18¹⁄₂}"

{7³⁄₄-8³⁄₄-8³⁄₄}{9-9-9¹⁄₄} {10¹⁄₄-10¹⁄₄-10³⁄₄}"

Note: Sweater includes two edge stitches.

Finished Afghan Size: 49" x 63"
(124.5 cm x 160 cm)

MATERIALS

Medium Weight Yarn **4** MEDIUM
[7 ounces, 364 yards
(198 grams, 333 meters) per skein]:
  7 skeins
  Note: Scrap yarn from other projects
    can be used for each Block.
Straight knitting needles, size 8
  (5 mm) **or** size needed for gauge

Basic patchwork afghans are made of forty-nine 7" x 9" (18 cm x 23 cm) rectangular blocks that are sewn together. Any pattern stitch can be used for the block.

GAUGE: In pattern,
        18 sts = 4" (10 cm);

MOSS PANELS BLOCK
Multiple of 8 + 7 sts.

Cast on 31 sts.

Row 1 (Right side)**:** Purl across.

Row 2: K3, (P1, K3) across.

Row 3: P3, (K1, P3) across.

Row 4: K2, P1, K1, P1, K2, ★ P1, K2, P1, K1, P1, K2; repeat from ★ 2 times **more**.

Row 5: P2, K1, P1, K1, P2, ★ K1, P2, K1, P1, K1, P2; repeat from ★ 2 times **more**.

Row 6: K1, (P1, K1) across.

Row 7: P1, (K1, P1) across.

Rows 8 and 9: Repeat Rows 4 and 5.

Rows 10 and 11: Repeat Rows 2 and 3.

Repeat Rows 2-11 until Block measures approximately 9" (23 cm) from cast on edge, ending by working a **right** side row.

Bind off all sts.

SEED STITCH ZIGZAG BLOCK
Multiple of 6 sts + 1.

Cast on 31 sts.

Row 1 (Right side)**:** Knit across.

Row 2: Purl across.

Row 3: P1, (K5, P1) across.

Row 4: P1, ★ K1, P3, K1, P1; repeat from ★ across.

Rows 5 and 6: P1, (K1, P1) across.

Row 7: K2, P1, K1, P1, ★ K3, P1, K1, P1; repeat from ★ across to last 2 sts, K2.

Row 8: P3, K1, (P5, K1) across to last 3 sts, P3.

Row 9: Knit across.

Row 10: Purl across.

Row 11: K3, P1, (K5, P1) across to last 3 sts, K3.

Row 12: P2, K1, P1, K1, ★ P3, K1, P1, K1; repeat from ★ across to last 2 sts, P2.

Rows 13 and 14: K1, (P1, K1) across.

Row 15: K1, ★ P1, K3, P1, K1; repeat from ★ across.

Row 16: K1, (P5, K1) across.

Repeat Rows 1-16 until Block measures approximately 9" (23 cm) from cast on edge, ending by working a **right** side row.

Bind off all sts in **knit**.

ASSEMBLY
Sew Blocks together, forming 7 vertical strips of 7 Blocks each and measuring 7" x 63" (18 cm x 160 cm). Sew strips together.

ABBREVIATIONS

cm	centimeters
K	knit
mm	millimeters
P	purl
PSSO	pass slipped stitch over
Rnd(s)	round(s)
SSK	slip, slip, knit
SSP	slip, slip, purl
st(s)	stitch(es)
tog	together
YO	yarn over

★ — work instructions following ★ as many **more** times as indicated in addition to the first time.

( ) or [ ] — work enclosed instructions **as many** times as specified by the number immediately following **or** contains explanatory remarks.

colon (:) — the number given after a colon at the end of a row or round denotes the number of stitches you should have on that row or round.

work even — work without increasing or decreasing in the established pattern.

KNITTING NEEDLES		
UNITED STATES	ENGLISH U.K.	METRIC (mm)
0	13	2
1	12	2.25
2	11	2.75
3	10	3.25
4	9	3.5
5	8	3.75
6	7	4
7	6	4.5
8	5	5
9	4	5.5
10	3	6
10½	2	6.5
11	1	8
13	00	9
15	000	10
17	---	12.75

Yarn Weight Symbol & Names	LACE 0	SUPER FINE 1	FINE 2	LIGHT 3	MEDIUM 4	BULKY 5	SUPER BULKY 6
Type of Yarns in Category	Fingering, size 10 crochet thread	Sock, Fingering, Baby	Sport, Baby	DK, Light Worsted	Worsted, Afghan, Aran	Chunky, Craft, Rug	Bulky, Roving
Knit Gauge Range* in Stockinette St to 4" (10 cm)	33-40** sts	27-32 sts	23-26 sts	21-24 sts	16-20 sts	12-15 sts	6-11 sts
Advised Needle Size Range	000-1	1 to 3	3 to 5	5 to 7	7 to 9	9 to 11	11 and larger

*GUIDELINES ONLY: The chart above reflects the most commonly used gauges and needle sizes for specific yarn categories.

** Lace weight yarns are usually knitted on larger needles to create lacy openwork patterns. Accordingly, a gauge range is difficult to determine. Always follow the gauge stated in your pattern.

KNIT TERMINOLOGY	
UNITED STATES	INTERNATIONAL
gauge =	tension
bind off =	cast off
yarn over (YO) =	yarn forward (yfwd) **or** yarn around needle (yrn)

■□□□ BEGINNER	Projects for first-time knitters using basic knit and purl stitches. Minimal shaping.	
■■□□ EASY	Projects using basic stitches, repetitive stitch patterns, simple color changes, and simple shaping and finishing.	
■■■□ INTERMEDIATE	Projects with a variety of stitches, such as basic cables and lace, simple intarsia, double-pointed needles and knitting in the round needle techniques, mid-level shaping and finishing.	
■■■■ EXPERIENCED	Projects using advanced techniques and stitches, such as short rows, fair isle, more intricate intarsia, cables, lace patterns, and numerous color changes.	

GAUGE

Exact gauge is **essential** for proper size. Before beginning your project, make a sample swatch in the yarn and needle specified in the individual instructions. After completing the swatch, measure it, counting your stitches and rows carefully. If your swatch is larger or smaller than specified, **make another, changing needle size to get the correct gauge**. Keep trying until you find the size needles that will give you the specified gauge. Once proper gauge is obtained, measure width of garment approximately every 3" (7.5 cm) to be sure gauge remains consistent.

MARKERS

As a convenience to you, we have used markers to mark the beginning of a round and to mark placement of increases. Place markers as instructed. You may use purchased markers or tie a length of contrasting color yarn around the needle. When you reach a marker, slip it from the left needle to the right needle; remove it when no longer needed.

ZEROS

To consolidate the length of an involved pattern, zeros are sometimes used so that all sizes can be combined. For example, increase every fourth row {3-1-0} time(s) means that the first size would increase 3 times, the second size would increase once, and the largest size would do nothing.

DOUBLE POINTED NEEDLES

The stitches are divided evenly between four double pointed needles as specified in the individual pattern. Form a square with the four needles. Do **not** twist the cast on ridge. With the remaining needle, work across the stitches on the first needle **(Fig. 1)**. You will now have an empty needle with which to work the stitches from the next needle. Work the first stitch of each needle firmly to prevent gaps. Continue working around without turning the work.

Fig. 1

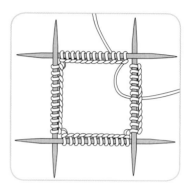

CIRCULAR KNITTING

When you knit in rounds, you are going to work around on the outside of the circle, with the right side of the knitting facing you.

Cast on the number of stitches indicated. Make sure the cast on ridge lays on the inside of the needle and never rolls around the needle **(Fig. 2a)**. Hold the needle so that the ball of yarn is attached to the stitch closest to the right hand point. Knit the stitches on the left hand point.

Fig. 2a

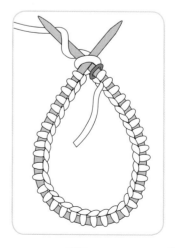

Since you need to use a shorter length needle then the measurement of stitches on your needle, it is sometimes necessary to use two circular needles at the same time.

The stitches are divided on two circular needles. Each needle is used independently of the other. While you are knitting across the first half of stitches with the other end of the same needle, the second needle will hang out of the way, with the stitches at the center of the cable. Then you will pick up both ends of the second needle, and work across it while the first needle hangs.

To begin, cast on the required number of stitches and slip the last half of stitches onto the second circular needle, placing them at the center of the cable *(Fig. 2b)*. Push the sts on the first needle to the tip at the other end. Move the first needle so that it is in front of and parallel to the cable of the second needle *(Fig. 2c)*. Holding both needles in your left hand, straighten your stitches so that they're not twisted around the needles.
When going from one needle to the next, keep the yarn between the first and last stitches snug to prevent a hole.
Using the other end of the same needle, work across the first needle.
Slide the stitches to the center of the cable and turn your work. Slide the stitches that are on the second needle from the cable to the point and work across *(Fig. 2d)*.
Continue in same manner.
A marker can be placed around any stitch to mark first needle.

Fig. 2b

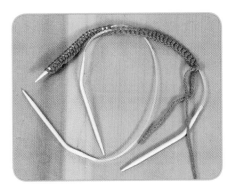

Fig. 2c

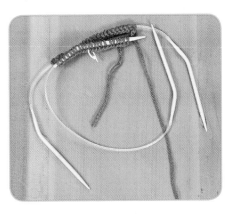

Fig. 2d

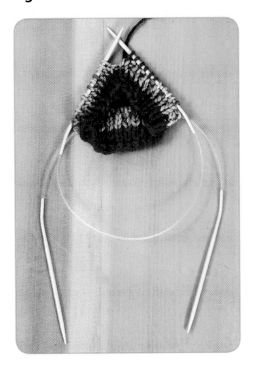

CROSS STITCHES
FRONT CROSS
Working in **front** of first stitch on left needle, knit second st *(Fig. 3a)* making sure **not** to drop off, then knit the first st *(Fig. 3b)* letting both sts drop off the needle.

Fig. 3a

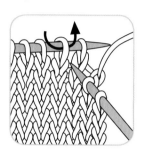

Fig. 3b

BACK CROSS
Working **behind** first st on left needle, knit into the back of second st *(Fig. 4a)* making sure **not** to drop off, then knit the first st *(Fig. 4b)* letting both sts drop off the needle.

Fig. 4a

Fig. 4b

PURL CROSS
Purl into the **front** of second st on left needle *(Fig. 5a)* making sure **not** to drop off, then purl the first st *(Fig. 5b)* letting both sts drop off the needle.

Fig. 5a

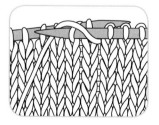

Fig. 5b

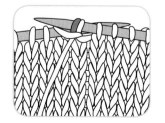

YARN OVERS *(abbreviated YO)*
After a knit stitch, before a knit stitch
Bring the yarn forward **between** the needles, then back **over** the top of the right hand needle, so that it is now in position to knit the next stitch *(Fig. 6a)*.

After a purl stitch, before a purl stitch
Take the yarn **over** the right hand needle to the back, then forward **under** it, so that it is now in position to purl the next stitch *(Fig. 6b)*.

Fig. 6a

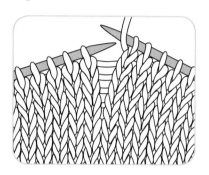

Fig. 6b

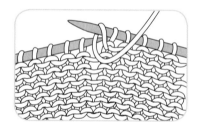

ADDING NEW STITCHES

Insert the right needle into the stitch as if to **knit**, yarn over and pull the loop through *(Fig. 7a)*, insert the left needle into the loop just worked from front to back and slip the loop onto the left needle *(Fig. 7b)*. Repeat for required number of stitches.

Fig. 7a

Fig. 7b

INCREASE

Knit the next stitch but do **not** slip the old stitch off the left needle *(Fig. 8a)*. Insert the right needle into the **back** loop of the **same** stitch and knit it *(Fig. 8b)*, then slip the old stitch off the left needle.

Fig. 8a

Fig. 8b

DECREASES
KNIT 2 TOGETHER *(abbreviated K2 tog)*

Insert the right needle into the **front** of the first two stitches on the left needle as if to **knit** *(Fig. 9)*, then **knit** them together as if they were one stitch.

Fig. 9

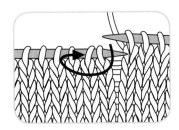

SLIP, SLIP, KNIT *(abbreviated SSK)*

Slip the first stitch as if to **knit**, then slip the next stitch as if to **knit** *(Fig. 10a)*. Insert the **left** needle into the **front** of both slipped stitches *(Fig. 10b)* and knit them together as if they were one stitch *(Fig. 10c)*.

Fig. 10a

Fig. 10b

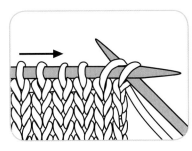

Fig. 10c

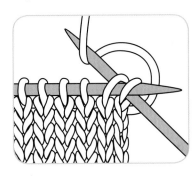

SLIP 1, KNIT 1, PASS SLIPPED STITCH OVER *(abbreviated slip 1, K1, PSSO)*

Slip one stitch as if to **knit** *(Fig. 10a)*. Knit the next stitch. With the left needle, bring the slipped stitch over the knit stitch *(Fig. 11)* and off the needle.

Fig. 11

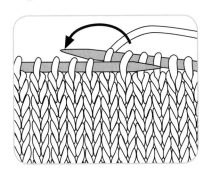

PURL 2 TOGETHER *(abbreviated P2 tog)*

Insert the right needle into the **front** of the first two stitches on the left needle as if to **purl** *(Fig. 12)*, then **purl** them together as if they were one stitch.

Fig. 12

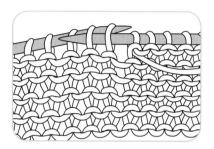

PURL 3 TOGETHER *(abbreviated P3 tog)*

Insert the right needle into the **front** of the first three stitches on the left needle as if to **purl** *(Fig. 13)*, then **purl** them together as if they were one stitch.

Fig. 13

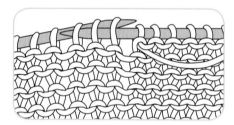

SLIP, SLIP, PURL *(abbreviated SSP)*

Slip the first stitch as if to **knit**, then slip the next stitch as if to **knit** *(Fig. 10a, page 75)*. Place these two stitches back onto the left needle. Insert the **right** needle into the **back** of both slipped stitches from the **back** to **front** *(Fig. 14)* and purl them together as if they were one stitch.

Fig. 14

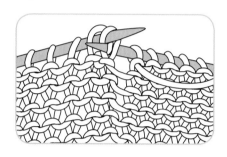

PICKING UP STITCHES

When instructed to pick up stitches, insert the needle from the **front** to the **back** under two strands at the edge of the worked piece *(Fig. 15a or b)*. Put the yarn around the needle as if to **knit**, then bring the needle with the yarn back through the stitch to the right side, resulting in a stitch on the needle.

Repeat this along the edge, picking up the required number of stitches.

A crochet hook may be helpful to pull yarn through.

Fig. 15a

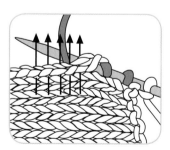

Fig. 15b

WEAVING SEAMS

With the **right** side of both pieces facing you and edges even, sew through both pieces once to secure the beginning of the seam, leaving an ample yarn end to weave in later. Insert the needle under the bar **between** the first and second stitches on the row and pull the yarn through *(Fig. 16)*. Insert the needle under the next bar on the second side. Repeat from side to side, being careful to match rows. If the edges are different lengths, it may be necessary to insert the needle under two bars at one edge.

Step 1: **Purl** first stitch on **front** needle, leave on *(Fig. 17a)*.
Step 2: **Knit** first stitch on **back** needle, leave on *(Fig. 17b)*.
Step 3: **Knit** first stitch on **front** needle, slip off.
Step 4: **Purl** next stitch on **front** needle, leave on.
Step 5: **Purl** first stitch on **back** needle, slip off.
Step 6: **Knit** next stitch on **back** needle, leave on.
Repeat Steps 3-6 across until all stitches are worked off the needles.

Fig. 16

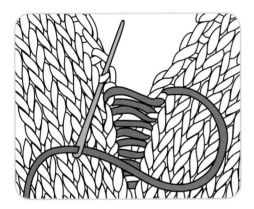

Fig. 17a

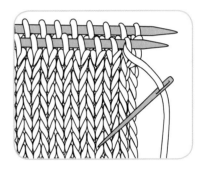

Fig. 17b

GRAFTING

Thread the yarn needle with the long end. Hold the threaded yarn needle on the right side of work.
Work in the following sequence, pulling yarn through as if to knit or as if to purl with even tension and keeping yarn under points of needles to avoid tangling and extra loops.

POM-POM

Cut a piece of cardboard 3" (7.5 cm) wide and as long as you want the diameter of your finished pom-pom to be.

Wind the yarn around the cardboard until it is approximately ½" (12 mm) thick in the middle *(Fig. 18a)*.

Carefully slip the yarn off the cardboard and firmly tie an 18" (45.5 cm) length of yarn around the middle *(Fig. 18b)*. Leave yarn ends long enough to attach the pom-pom. Cut the loops on both ends and trim the pom-pom into a smooth ball *(Fig. 18c)*.

Fig. 18b

Fig. 18c

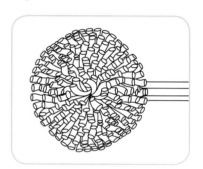

Fig. 18a

yarn information

The projects in this leaflet were made using a variety of yarns. Any brand in the specified weight may be used. It is best to refer to the yardage/meters when determining how many skeins or hanks to purchase. Remember, to arrive at the finished size, it is the GAUGE/TENSION that is important, not the brand of yarn. For your convenience, listed below are the specific yarns used to create our photography models.

CUFFED HAT
Cascade Yarns, Cascade 220
#7813 Jade

HELMET LINER
Red Heart® Super Saver®
#4365 Coffee Fleck

HUG CAP
TLC® Cotton Plus™
#3590 Lavender

HOODED SCARF
Red Heart® Soft Baby Steps™
Main Color - #9800
Baby Blue
Contrasting Color - #9932
Puppy Print

SCARF
Moda Dea® Washable Wool™
Main Color - #4435 Taupe
Color A - #4440 Moss
Color B - #4439
Charcoal Grey

MITTENS
Red Heart® Super Saver®
Solid pair - #512 Turqua
Variegated pair - #928
Earth & Sky

SLIPPERS
Red Heart® Super Saver®
#256 Carrot

THICK SOCKS
Cascade Yarns, Cascade 220
#8901 Groseille

SOCKS
Bernat® Sox
#42013 Desert Storm

CHILD'S VEST
Cascade Yarns, Cascade 220
#2413 Cherry Red

INFANT'S PULLOVER
Moda Dea® Washable Wool™
#4423 Aqua

T-SWEATER
Lion Brand® Vanna's Choice®
#144 Magenta

CHILD'S SWEATER
Moda Dea® Washable Wool™
Main Color - #4473
Rose Pink
Contrasting Color - #4431
Plum

MARINER'S VEST
TLC® Heathers™
#2443 Nutmeg

BABY BLANKET
Caron® Simply Soft® Brites
#9609 Berry Blue

AFGHAN
Lion Brand® Lion® Wool
#132 Lemongrass

ANIMAL'S BLANKET
Red Heart® Super Saver®
#320 Cornmeal

BULKY SWEATER
Patons® Classic Wool
#77010 Natural Marl

WARM UP AMERICA BLOCKS
Red Heart® Super Saver®
#774 Lt Raspberry
#530 Orchid

a word from
LEISURE ARTS
and MIRA books

LOOK FOR DEBBIE'S HEARTWARMING STORIES AT BOOKSTORES EVERYWHERE, AND COLLECT ALL NINE OF HER KNITTING PUBLICATIONS!

knit along with
DEBBIE MACOMBER

Read The Books that Inspired the Projects

Cedar Cove Series

Item# 4658

Inspired by Debbie's popular Blossom Street and Cedar Cove book series, the *Knit Along with Debbie Macomber* companion books are a treasure trove of patterns to knit! And have you discovered the classic patterns in *Debbie's Favorites* or the thoughtful designs in *Friendship Shawls*? Take time to indulge yourself with Debbie's warm and memorable tales; then treat yourself to a little creativity from Leisure Arts!

Other Debbie Macomber Publications

Item# 4692

Item# 4504

Item# 4803

LEISURE ARTS®
the art of everyday living

To find out more about Debbie Macomber, visit www.debbiemacomber.com or www.mirabooks.com.

For information about these and other Leisure Arts publications, call 1.800.526.5111 or visit www.leisurearts.com.